Praise for

Lead Like Jael

"*Lead Like Jael* is pure gospel gold, a beautifully written book that champions feminine strength and greatness through Christ-wrought submission. Emma Waters calls all Christian women—maidens, mothers, and matriarchs—to lead deep, purposeful lives filled with wisdom. This accessible and wise book outlines a strategy for women at all stages of life to pursue a biblically grounded home economy in which faith, marriage, and children come first. Buy a copy for every woman in your life!"

—**Rosaria Butterfield**, wife, mother, and author of *The Secret Thoughts of an Unlikely Convert*, *The Gospel Comes with a House Key*, and *Five Lies of Our Anti-Christian Age*

"Emma Waters challenges the polarizing roles now offered to women. *Lead Like Jael* masterfully strips away these limits and helps us reexamine the power of our role in light of Scripture and discernment. Motherhood becomes a holy calling coupled with spiritual warfare (Psalm 127:4), your husband is your ally in battle, and your dinner table becomes an altar. You are going to want a copy for yourself and your daughter."

—**Lisa Bevere**, *New York Times* bestselling author of *Without Rival* and cofounder of Messenger International

"While the US is in the midst of declining marriage and birth rates, when 'self' everything is the mantra of the age, Emma invites you to 'recover a biblical vision of womanhood rooted in faithfulness to Christ above all.' Truly, this is the abundant life."

—**Congresswoman Mary Miller**, representing the Fifteenth District of Illinois

"Today's marketplace of ideas for women seems to be narrowly defined by two extremes: the girl boss or the tradwife. Emma Waters, through rich and concrete examples, biblical heroines, and contemporary research, offers a much broader and healthier understanding of how we can live, lead, and love. *Lead Like Jael* offers women a model we all need but didn't know existed."

—**Dr. Carrie Gress**, author of *Something Wicked* and *Theology of Home*

"*Lead Like Jael* is a bracing, much-needed corrective to a quiet but corrosive trend within the modern church—the uncritical absorption of feminist assumptions that recast women's flourishing in terms of autonomy, careerism, and self-actualization rather than covenant, obedience, and fruitfulness. With clarity and conviction, Emma Waters restores a biblical vision of womanhood rooted in Scripture rather than cultural fashion. For readers seeking an antidote to feminism's quiet theological drift—and a compelling vision of womanhood that is joyful, disciplined, and rooted in God's design—this book is both timely and necessary."

—**Megan Basham**, *New York Times* bestselling author of *Shepherds for Sale: How Evangelical Leaders Traded the Truth for a Leftist Agenda* and culture reporter for The Daily Wire

"This book is a stake in the ground—or a tent peg!—for Christian femininity. Emma has mined the wisdom of our biblical foremothers to paint a practical and inviting picture of living a full and joy-filled life as a woman of God in *our* moment. Every young woman, and every 'matriarch' mentoring them, needs to read this."

—**Maria Baer**, journalist and cohost of the *Breakpoint This Week* podcast with the Colson Center

"In *Lead Like Jael*, Emma Waters points out a path to women that runs between girl-boss feminism and the tradwife movement. This is a path that honors marriage and family, that upholds the dignity of all human life, that advances the common good, and that allows women to use the gifts they uniquely bring to public and private life. Waters is a singularly important new voice in today's conversation about women, men, family, and the pursuit of justice."

—**W. Brad Wilcox,** Distinguished University Professor of Sociology at the University of Virginia and author of *Get Married: Why Americans Must Defy the Elites, Forge Strong Families, and Save Civilization*

"Every word Emma Waters writes radiates with beautiful, shimmering truth. She brilliantly compares powerful feminine examples from the Bible, like the righteous Jael, with modern-day women suffering under the self-inflicted lies of progressive feminism. Fascinating and insightful, the book itself is a sharp stake through the heart of the movement that has sought to subjugate us with decades of indoctrination. Emma understands like few young women do that victory in this fight will require us to channel some of the Old Testament heroine Jael's implacable female bravery—and see our enemies for what they are. 'God is within her, she will not fall.' Emma Waters has written a book I wish someone had given me years ago, and one that all faithful women should own."

—**Peachy Keenan,** author of *Domestic Extremist: A Practical Guide to Winning the Culture War*

LEAD LIKE
JAEL

LEAD LIKE JAEL

7 Timeless Principles for Today's Women of Faith

EMMA WATERS

Regnery Faith books may be purchased in bulk at special discounts for sales promotion, corporate gifts, fund-raising, or educational purposes. Special editions can also be created to specifications. For details, contact the Special Sales Department, Regnery Faith, 307 Fifth Avenue, 4th Floor, New York, NY 10016 or info@skyhorsepublishing.com.

Regnery Faith™ is an imprint of Skyhorse Publishing, Inc.®, a Delaware corporation.

Visit our website at www.regnery.com.
Please follow our publisher Tony Lyons on Instagram @tonylyonsisuncertain.

10 9 8 7 6 5 4 3 2 1

Library of Congress Cataloging-in-Publication Data is available on file.

Cover design by David Ter-Avanesyan
Cover image by Shutterstock

Print ISBN: 978-1-5107-8353-9
Ebook ISBN: 978-1-5107-8542-7

Printed in the United States of America

To Elisabeth Elliot, a true matriarch in the faith whose faithfulness as a Christian, missionary, wife, mother, and friend continues to bless and encourage each generation of women.

***

The Lord God is with me, and that alone makes all the difference.

CONTENTS

PREFACE

Putting First Things First

"Can you believe that we're here?" Madeline asked over lunch one afternoon in Washington, DC.

I was gently rocking Cordelia, my youngest at the time, in her stroller, trying to keep her settled while Madeline and I caught up. Madeline was one of the first friends I made when I moved to Washington, DC, in 2021, and we quickly bonded over shared values, homeschool experiences, and our love for hosting. We were enjoying one of our rare but treasured lunch hangouts during one of my monthly visits to the city. Though I had lived in DC for four years, I was only coming back for work once a month, working remotely the rest of the time while my husband finished seminary in Pennsylvania.

"No," I replied. "If you had told me five years ago that I'd be here, I never would have believed it."

Five years ago, I was having an absolute meltdown over the thought of becoming a mother. I was convinced it would derail my career ambitions and leave me sad, alone, and irrelevant. (Though honestly, what does it even mean to be "relevant"?) I was so afraid that I broke up with my then-boyfriend, Jack, right as we were talking about marriage because the idea of beginning life as a wife and mother felt like a major letdown after years of working hard in college to prepare for a career in politics.

I was on the edge of winning valedictorian, had earned top awards, and was eagerly planning to move to DC. I can't fully explain it now, but fear convinced me that motherhood would be the end of my dreams and everything I had worked so hard to achieve. I knew God was calling me to a great and impactful future, and children felt like a hindrance and distraction.

That fear snowballed into a summer of tense conversations and eventually led me to break up with Jack on a whim, despite a whirlwind romance and real hopes of marriage in the near future. I cried the entire day trying to make sense of what I had just done.

I'd broken up with men before; that wasn't new. I'd been broken up with, too. But this time felt different. The longer it sat, the more the pit in my stomach grew into something like a black hole. What had I been thinking?

In hindsight, my fearful decision failed the test of wisdom on every count. What first felt like clarity actually was emotional confusion, spiritual disorientation, and the absence of discernment. Looking back, the decision bore all the markers of biblical foolishness.

Markers of a Foolish Decision:

1. Trusting in Myself Instead of the Fear of the Lord
   "The fear of the Lord is the beginning of wisdom, and the knowledge of the Holy One is insight" (Proverbs 9:10). In the fog of confusion, I dressed up my decision with spiritual language to mask a fearful heart that wasn't seeking God's will as much as my own escape.

2. Made in Haste Without Seeking Wise Counsel
   "The plans of the diligent lead surely to abundance, but everyone who is hasty comes only to poverty" (Proverbs 21:5). A wise decision is marked by patience and preparation; mine was rushed, fueled by fear rather than prayer or wise counsel.
3. Driven by Emotion over Discernment
   "A fool takes no pleasure in understanding, but only in expressing his opinion" (Proverbs 18:2). I acted impulsively, giving more weight to my internal panic than to thoughtful reflection or godly understanding.
4. Ignoring Red Flags and Warnings
   "The prudent sees danger and hides himself, but the simple go on and suffer for it" (Proverbs 27:12). In my determination to protect my future, I ignored both my own unease and the gentle attempts of those who loved me to slow down and consider my actions.
5. Prioritizing Immediate Relief over Long-Term Faithfulness
   "There is a way that seems right to a man, but its end is the way to death" (Proverbs 14:12). Breaking off the relationship gave me a fleeting sense of control but left me with a lingering ache and deep regret.

The Bible consistently teaches that wisdom comes from fearing the Lord, seeking His guidance, and being humble enough to learn from our mistakes and the guidance of others. Foolishness, on the other hand, is marked by pride, impulsiveness, and disobeying God's Word.

I was miserable.

At first, I tried to throw myself into my work by focusing on policy research, writing projects, and speaking opportunities. On paper, it was everything I had worked for and dreamed of. But something was missing. I began to realize that even the most exciting projects—the kind that had once made me feel ambitious and alive—suddenly felt flat. Without the hope of building something meaningful for the future, my work felt hollow.

But the damage had been done. After I broke his heart, Jack wasn't about to take me back on a whim.

I wasn't sure what else to do, so I reached out to my high school youth pastor, Victor, and poured out my heart. I was raw, emotional, and full of regret. He listened patiently and helped me draft a letter, which I sent just two or three weeks after the breakup. In it, I confessed how I had let dreams of grandeur cloud my judgment and how deeply I regretted my decision.

I didn't ask Jack to take me back. At least, not directly. I simply said I wanted to consider getting back together. His reply came quickly and coolly: a noncommittal but polite "message received." He wasn't angry, but he certainly wasn't chasing me either. And I knew then that I had work to do. I still had a lot of unanswered questions about marriage, motherhood, and the role of work in my life.

I couldn't just waltz back into the life of someone I had seriously discussed marriage with. If I wanted to rebuild trust, it would take time, humility, and intentional growth.

It's worth noting that Jack had never pressured me into motherhood or demanded that I quit work. He didn't hand down ultimatums. But he was clear-headed and principled. He openly admired the childhood his mother gave him as a stay-at-home mom and hoped to offer that same gift to his future children. He never minimized my ambitions, but he also didn't idolize them. Jack had the strength and steadiness to hold space for my confusion without capitulating to it. And in hindsight, I realized how rare and how wise that was.

The first time I seriously thought about marriage and motherhood, I did so with a self-centered lens: What do I want? What will this cost me? I began with my desires rather than with the Bible. This time, though, something had changed. I wasn't just trying to justify a preference.

I genuinely wanted to know: What does the Bible actually say about marriage, motherhood, children, ambition, calling, and meaningful work? Could these pieces fit together in a way that honored God and made sense of my longings? I was finally ready to find out.

In my case, I was afraid that children (or at least having children sooner rather than much later) would hold me back from my own personal growth and career. Somehow, I had gotten this idea that prioritizing marriage and children earlier in life is what you do if you lack ambition. (This couldn't be further from the truth.)

A mentor in that season faithfully pointed out to me that the Bible talks about children very differently. Not only does the Bible say that children are a blessing from the Lord, but motherhood is one of the most profound ways that God refines us and calls us to maturity. I've heard Eastern Orthodox Christians call marriage a "fast track to theosis" (becoming like God), and motherhood is even more so as women give their body and blood to bring new life into the world. Taken together, my mentor summarized it well: Either you're right or God's Word is right, but these cannot both be true.

So when I began studying the Bible on its own terms, what I found surprised me.

Women in the Bible couldn't be flattened into one-dimensional labels like "just a mother." Figures such as Mary, Rahab, Sarah, Jael, Deborah, and the wise women of Tekoa and Abel weren't praised for stepping outside of their roles; they were honored because they lived faithfully within them.

The Bible described children as covenantal signs and living evidence of God's ongoing promises to us. Biblical women didn't treat children as obstacles to their purpose. They fought for and alongside their children and shaped history by faithfully raising them.

Jesus said, "The thief comes only to steal and kill and destroy. I came that they may have life and have it abundantly" (John 10:10). That truth finally began to click for me. The real foolishness wasn't just in breaking up with Jack; it was in believing the enemy's lies that God's laws were not His best for me.

God wasn't withholding something from me; He was offering me my best yes. A harder yes, perhaps. One that would involve sacrifice, growth, and moments of disappointment. But one that would also bring joy, contentment, and a purpose far greater than I could imagine. Indeed, God's good design for the family is not only good, but for my good.

It was then that the Lord taught me a powerful lesson about putting first things first.

After three months apart (it might as well have been three years!), Jack and I agreed to meet at the end of our semester to talk.

We set the date several weeks in advance. During that time, I was busy applying for internships, finally landing a solid offer after weeks of silence. I interviewed, they made an offer, and I accepted—only to learn that I would be required to attend mandatory training in Texas.

The training fell on the exact weekend that Jack and I had set aside to meet. There was no way to do both. I had to choose. The poetic justice of it wasn't lost on me.

This time, I chose Jack. As we left college for Christmas break, we met to discuss our time apart, the lessons we had learned, and whether there was still hope for a future together. I shared everything God had been teaching me about marriage and motherhood, and how I had chosen that conversation with Jack even above career advancement.

Two days after Jack and I met, two of the top internship organizations in my field reached out with offers for positions in departments I had only dreamed of joining. Not only did I end up with better opportunities than I had initially pursued, but I was also able to accept both. I had given up what I thought was the only open door, and in return, God opened two even better ones. I received more than I could have asked for or imagined.

As C. S. Lewis wisely said, "Put first things first and we get second things thrown in: put second things first and we lose both first and second things."[1] When we honor God's design and seek His kingdom above all else, everything else falls into place in unexpected ways.

And so, Jack and I got back together. It wasn't easy. Rebuilding trust, working through past wounds, and learning to communicate with grace took, and still takes, real effort. Seven months later, we were engaged. Now, after several years of marriage, two beautiful daughters, and a life rich with joy and sanctification, I can see how God continues to bless our obedience. Not because He has to, or because we are perfect, but because He is a good Father who delights in giving good gifts to His children.

That pattern has occurred multiple times in my life. Every time I take a "step back" professionally to prioritize our growing family, bigger opportunities come. Whether it's working early hours to be present with our daughters while they're awake or working remotely while my husband pursues full-time seminary, newer and bigger opportunities have come my way.

That afternoon with Madeline in DC felt like a full-circle moment. The girl who once feared that marriage and motherhood would derail her life now sat across the table, a stroller by her side, marveling at the goodness of God. I couldn't have scripted the path that led there, but His grace had carried me through every doubt, detour, and hard decision.

Growing up, I was raised in a Christian home, read my Bible weekly, played an active role in my church, and attended a Christian college. And yet without even realizing it, I had adopted the world's model of success, and in doing so, I risked missing out on all the blessings of marriage and motherhood.

I got one thing right during that fear-filled season: marriage, and especially motherhood, does require me to die to myself. Fully. Completely. But when we die with Christ, we are also resurrected with Him in fullness of life.

It's like that scene in C. S. Lewis's The Voyage of the Dawn Treader when Eustace Scrubb, who had been turned into a dragon by his own greed and stubbornness, tried in vain to peel off his thick, scaly skin. Layer after layer came off, but he couldn't get deep enough to solve the problem himself. Then Aslan stepped in. It hurt as the great Lion tore away the dragon skin, but when it was over, Eustace was free and restored to the boy he was always meant to be. That picture has stayed with me. Marriage, motherhood, and life with Christ have all been like that for me. As God stripped away the selfishness I could never remove on my own, He uncovered a surprising freedom and joy underneath.

The book you're holding is, in many ways, the fruit of my early life shaped by lessons learned, suffering endured, and the hard-won truths I wish someone had imparted to me in college.

My prayer is that as you read, you will discover the same freedom, joy, and abundant life I found in learning how to put first things first.

INTRODUCTION

The Rise of the Tradwife

The girl boss is dead. Long live the tradwife.

For much of the last century, progress for women meant movement out of the home and into the workforce. From Rosie the Riveter in the 1940s, to the career women of the 1980s, and finally to the "girl boss" of the 2010s, female empowerment was increasingly framed in economic and individualistic terms: more freedom, more earning power, more sexual liberation, and more visibility in male-dominated spaces.

To be a modern woman was to want *more.*

But by the time the 2020s arrived, ushered in with the global COVID-19 pandemic, the narrative began to falter. The once-celebrated "girl boss"—a symbol of a self-starting, career-driven woman who leaned in, broke glass ceilings, and curated her #hustle on Instagram—was losing her shine. In her place, a more domestic figure emerged from the edges of TikTok and Instagram: the "tradwife," or the traditional wife. Cotton aprons replaced pantsuits, baking bread replaced attending business meetings, and a soft and receptive femininity was no longer taboo but increasingly admired.

The Fall of Girl-Boss Feminism

The peak of girl-boss feminism arguably came in 2019. A century after the Nineteenth Amendment granted women the right to vote, *Politico* declared 2019 "The Year of the Woman."[1] By all appearances, it was a triumphant moment for modern feminism. Media outlets cheered as women reached the highest levels of politics, business, and academia.

During President Donald Trump's State of the Union Address that year, he received a bipartisan standing ovation when he celebrated that more women were in the workforce than ever before.[2] A then-record number of women had been elected to serve in Congress.[3] NASA, Nike, and universities across the country spotlighted female achievements in their fields. Girl-boss feminism had succeeded in reframing womanhood around metrics once reserved for men: titles, salaries, influence, and independence. The movement seemed unstoppable.

Then, something unexpected happened: the world shut down.

The COVID-19 pandemic delivered what no amount of cultural critique could: a global chill pill. It was the ultimate permission slip for women to return to their homes and children—or to face the reality of life without marriage or children head on. Even before this, though, the rate of antidepressant use "went up 400 perfect over a 10-year period"[4] with women twice as likely to take such medication than men.[5] While 16.5 percent of women overall were taking such medication for depression, anxiety, and loneliness,[6] 23 percent of women between the ages of forty and fifty-nine were in 2016.[7] Despite having more freedom, education, and economic power than any generation before them, many women felt something important was missing.

Girl-boss feminism, a modern, career-obsessed take on womanhood, celebrated individual ambition and corporate success, often at the cost of marriage, motherhood, and community. It told women that their value lay in their productivity and professional titles, rather than in their faith, family, and God-given identity. These women were told they could have it all, only to discover that "all" was not enough.

While a 2024 report from the Pew Research Center found that "69% of those who have never been married say they want to get married one day,"[8] only about 53 percent of adults in the United States are married,[9] the CDC found that birth rates were at an all-time low in 2024,[10] and in the second wave of the US Adult Sexual Behaviors and Attitudes Study from March 2021, 37 percent of US adults—whether already parents or not—reported that they wished they had more children.[11]

The pandemic exposed this dissonance with sudden clarity. Offices shuttered, daycare centers closed, and schools went remote. Women were, quite literally, sent home. And to the surprise of many, some didn't want to leave again—or, at least not in the way they had before. Flexible work, part-time jobs, and stay-at-home motherhood have continued to see a resurgence as many women decided that it makes more sense, either financially or emotionally, to stay home with their young children.

Like a chicken with its head cut off, girl-boss feminism may still be making headlines, but the life has gone out of it. The girl boss failed. She championed abortion, autonomy, and winning the battle of the sexes—placing herself above children, career above family, and freedom above responsibility. She rejected limits, and in doing so, she lost herself. Her downfall isn't a tragedy; it's a necessary end.

The Rise of the Tradwife Movement

The tradwife movement exploded in 2020, drawing millions of followers to influencers who embraced homesteading, homemade meals, soft femininity, and traditional gender roles. Articles like "'Tradwives': The New Trend for Submissive Women Has a Dark Heart and History" in

The Guardian, "Help! Am I Becoming an Accidental #Tradwife?" in *Refinery29*, and "The Rise and Fall of the Tradwife" in *The New Yorker* all wrestled with the trend's meaning.[12] As Brittany Hugoboom, the founder of *Evie Magazine*, observed in her *Washington Examiner* essay "Hell Hath No Fury Like a Feminist Witnessing a Beautiful Woman Living Her Dreams," the tradwife image touched a nerve and revealed how deep the cultural divide had become between these competing life scripts for women.[13]

I was initially critical of the tradwife movement as it appeared online. I even drafted a few articles, thankfully never published, before realizing my frustration might be missing the point. Sure, there were accounts that felt like caricatures: women in cinched-waist dresses, hair in perfect vintage curls, and red lipstick always on hand, while declaring that their husband "didn't have to lift a finger in the home." Many embraced a romanticized 1950s ideal, offering listicles that sounded something like "10 Ways to Be a Submissive Wife" or "8 Things Tradwives Never Do." Some accounts were deeply religious, while others were simply disillusioned with the false promises of modern feminism.

Despite the tradwife's general rejection of paid work outside the home, it struck me that these women were not reacting against *work* itself, but against a system that told them their worth was measured by career success. In this way, the movement is not so much a return to the 1950s or another bygone era but is an indictment of the 2010s: years marked by weakened families distrustful of predatory and self-seeking financial and political movements and a corporatized feminism that no longer spoke to women's real needs.

Despite the attention-seeking nature of some of its representatives, the tradwife movement clearly was addressing a felt need in the modern woman. The popularity of the movement suggests that the project of female liberation is incomplete—and in many cases, headed in the wrong direction. It shows us the unfulfilled dreams many women long for: homes that are alive with meaningful labor, marriages that are strong, children who are cherished, and a life that aligns with what we value most.

Even Gloria Steinem, now in her nineties and a feminist leader of the sexual revolution in the twentieth century, has recognized the centrality of the home for women's success in this cultural and political moment. "The lesson is less in the national and world atmosphere and more in the home and employment atmosphere in which we have some control," she said in a *New York Times* article published after the 2024 presidential election. "We shouldn't give up the power we have."[14]

Still, it must be said again that the tradwife movement is not the ultimate solution to our cultural malaise. At its worst, it can veer into "live-action role-play" or legalism. The temptation to curate a life rather than live it is strong—especially among the millions of women who consume tradwife content without taking meaningful steps toward wisdom, marriage, motherhood, or aspects of homemaking. And without a grounding in biblical wisdom, even the most beautiful domestic life can become a white-washed tomb.

This is why it is a mistake to treat the *tradwife* as the antidote to the *girl boss*. Both present a narrow view of womanhood. The girl-boss model idolizes professional achievement and individualism; the tradwife model reinforces an individualized and false binary between the public and private spheres that is already rampant in our culture today. Try as it might, the tradwife model does not treat the root causes of our cultural loneliness and emptiness.

It's striking that the questions women are now asking about hustle culture echo the very ones posed by second-wave feminists, such as Betty Friedan in her 1963 book *The Feminine Mystique*: "Each suburban wife struggles with it alone. As she made the beds, shopped for groceries, matched slipcover material, ate peanut butter sandwiches with her children, chauffeured Cub Scouts and Brownies, lay beside her husband at night—she was afraid to ask even of herself the silent question: 'Is this all?'"[15] Except instead of the home, this feeling of emptiness is coming from within the walls of corporate culture.

One could even reframe Friedan's question, as I have done here, to reflect the emptiness of hustle culture: Each working mother bears it alone. As she answered emails between meetings, juggled deadlines and daycare pickups, ate a rushed lunch at her desk while drafting presentations no one would remember, joined late-night conference calls while folding laundry, scrolled through pictures of the kids she barely saw that week, lay beside her husband at night—she was afraid to ask even of herself the silent question: *"Is this all?"*

Friedan aimed her critique at the constraints of domestic life in the mid-twentieth century. Yet sixty years later, women are asking the same question about the restless, career-driven culture Friedan helped inspire.

Crafting a Home Economy, not a New Ideology

A neatly packaged femininity rooted in a 1950s June Cleaver ideal may be easy to sell, but as journalist and author Mary Harrington argues in her incisive *UnHerd* article "Why the Tradwives Aren't Trad Enough," it's not really traditional. What many tradwife influencers offer is not the way most decades structured the home, but a repackaged version of modernity—one that, in her words, "literally, drove women insane."[16] Before industrialization, households were collaborative economies where husbands and wives worked side by side through craft, farming, or trade. The 1950s split the home from the economy, dividing men's and women's work in ways foreign to earlier generations.

In place of the tradwife, Harrington proposes a revival of the *tradewife*: women who participate in family-centered home economies. "From this point of view," Harrington concludes, "the way forward might be less 'tradwife' than 'tradewife.'"[17] And the numbers suggest many mothers may want that, too. In 2019, a Gallup poll found that over 50 percent of moms with kids under eighteen say they'd prefer to stay home.[18] And, in 2021, an American Compass survey found that "a full-time, stay-at-home parent is the most popular arrangement across lower-, working-, and middle-class respondents," with one report published with the Institute for Family showing that 63 percent of married moms call part-time or no work the ideal.[19] Still, 74 percent remain in the workforce or are looking for work, according to the US Bureau of Labor Statistics.[20] The question, then, is how we might redesign work, family life, and education to make this integrated vision more possible.

This model animates the best examples of the movement, often by women who forgo the tradwife label altogether. Take, for example, Hannah Neeleman of Ballerina Farm, a Juilliard-trained ballerina, 2023 Mrs. American winner, co-owner of a multi-million-dollar business, and mother of eight. Or model and influencer Nara Smith, who is known for her raspy-voiced reels documenting her elaborate meals made from scratch. Both women have built productive home economies alongside their husbands and children. They aren't rejecting modernity, technology, or work but are integrating them into lives where their marriage and children come first.

Nara, in particular, frames motherhood as foundational rather than a detour. "I want to build my life with them [my children] rather than trying to integrate them into my life later," she said in an interview with *GQ*. "And it worked out great. I love being a young mom."[21] Nara's vision of building life around home and family rather than fitting them into the margins reflects the longing of many women today.

Why I Wrote *Lead Like Jael*

Some women will remain in the workforce. Others will step away from it. Still more will choose a middle path that allows them to prioritize their families while also earning an income, building businesses, or pursuing creative work.

In truth, most women already live in this middle space. They work, either out of necessity or desire, yet struggle to place their homes and relationships first. Like many in the tradwife movement, they sense that family life and the well-being of their children must take precedence over the relentless demands of careerism.

Rather than relying on abstract arguments, feminist jargon, or the romanticized imagery of the tradwife movement, this book seeks to uncover the deeper *why* behind women's longings to live strong, purposeful lives. It takes this cultural moment and the angst revealed in hustle culture and tradwife ideals and places it within a truer framework: the wisdom of the Bible and the call of Lady Wisdom herself.

And this is where the Christian vision offers something different altogether. The longings that draw women to hustle culture and the tradwife aesthetic find their true answer not in either extreme but in Christ, the fulfillment of wisdom, who reorders our loves, labor, and life. The answer to Friedan's haunting question, whether whispered in the suburbs of the 1960s or in the office towers and on Instagram, is the same: *Is this all?* Scripture answers with a resounding no.

Still, many young women are holding on tight to career-first ideals. An NBC Decision Desk poll found that among Gen Z women who voted for former vice president Kamala Harris during the 2024 presidential election, the top marker of success was "having a job or career you find fulfilling," while being married and having children ranked near the bottom.[22] Even among women who voted for Donald Trump, career fulfillment was second only to financial independence, far above marriage or children.[23] For Trump-voting men, however, "having children" came first. The data suggest men are rethinking success around family, while many women still measure it by career.[24]

Today, women are starving for a strong and inspiring vision of what it means to be a woman that engages her fullest potential *as a woman.*

What if we told this generation of women that home, marriage, and children are not a barrier to meaningful engagement, but a gate? What if we taught them that these primary relationships of husband and children refine and strengthen them for successful work in political, social, religious, and personal realms—either directly, or through their husband and children?

What if we painted a picture of a biblically grounded home economy where faith, marriage, and children come first? A vision where service to family and community stands as the highest calling, yet is one that also draws on a woman's full range of gifts, including her strength, intellect, creativity, and ambition, woven together for God's glory and the good of others.

Too often, women enter adulthood armed with cultural scripts that do not fit. Like King Saul's preparations for David to fight Goliath, the armor does not fit, the sword is awkward, and it just doesn't feel right. Why? Because God equipped women to fight in a distinct way that corresponds with their natural abilities, gifts, and strengths.

That is why I wrote *Lead Like Jael*—to recover the pursuit of Lady Wisdom in an age of competing identities and shallow scripts. Drawing from the lives of biblical women, each chapter traces how God calls women to build, nurture, defend, and lead with strength rooted in Him. Together, they form what I call the "Tent Peg Strategy," a model for faithful, courageous leadership in a world desperate for both.

The Tent Peg Strategy

There's a concept in marketing called the *tentpole* strategy, and my understanding is that it revolves around having one big idea or selling point around which everything else is built. Lose that center, and the whole tent collapses.

This book follows a similar pattern but with a twist: it offers a *tent peg* strategy, in honor of Jael's iconic tool. At the center stands Lady Wisdom, the pole that holds everything upright. Yet a tent needs more than a center post. Seven stakes secure the edges, each one essential for keeping the structure steady. Leave one loose, and the canvas starts to flap or cave, threatening the whole tent.

The seven tent pegs, which correspond with each of the seven principles, are these:

1. **Discernment:** Seeing clearly what is true, good, and right—even when culture, emotions, or circumstances cloud the way.
2. **Shrewdness:** Applying prudence, strategy, and courage to protect life, expose evil, and advance God's promises and people.
3. **Resourcefulness:** Using the tools, skills, and responsibilities God has given to stand firm, act wisely, and let ordinary obedience become the foundation for extraordinary impact.
4. **Life-Giving Hospitality:** Opening our homes, setting our tables, and creating space to care for the physical, spiritual, and emotional needs of those around us, where simple acts of obedience become God's means of reconciliation, unmasking evil, and bringing new life.
5. **Marriage on Mission:** Restoring husbands and wives as battlemates rather than rivals, rejecting the cultural script that pits men and women against each other and embracing a shared calling to build God's kingdom together in the home, church, and community.
6. **Motherhood as Warfare:** Motherhood grows women in influence and strength as they disciple, discipline, and launch children to follow God faithfully, making it both a spiritual calling and a force for good in the world.

7. **Wise Counsel and Negotiation:** As spiritual matriarchs, older faithful women guide families, churches, and communities with discernment, courage, and godly wisdom.

When one of these stakes is missing or weak, things begin to collapse. Without discernment, women fall for smooth-talkers or false ideologies that twist good and evil. Without shrewdness, they trust the wrong people or justify manipulation. Lacking resourcefulness, they neglect the ordinary duties through which God often works His greatest victories. Without hospitality, homes become pit stops for busy schedules, meals become hurried or solitary, and tables meant for conversation and connection fall silent before screens. When marriage loses its mission, it drifts toward apathy, divorce, or self-centered and separate pursuits. Without a view of motherhood as warfare and a beautiful extension of one's life, children become optional or secondary priorities. And when wise counsel disappears, families and communities lose the older women who once mediated conflicts, offered guidance in crises, and steadied entire nations with prayerful presence and practical wisdom.

But these seven pegs only hold firm when they are anchored in *Lady Wisdom*, the biblical image of wisdom who ultimately finds her fulfillment in Jesus Christ. In Proverbs, Wisdom is personified as a woman who calls out in the streets, inviting all to walk in understanding and to build their lives on what is true and good. The Apostle Paul later reveals that Jesus Himself is "the power of God and the wisdom of God" (1 Corinthians 1:24). In Him, the beauty and strength of Lady Wisdom are made complete.

Like Jael directing the tent peg that secured victory for Israel, wise women today fasten their homes and their hearts to Christ, the true Wisdom. Rooted in Him, they plant each stake deeply, building families, communities, and legacies that can endure even the fiercest storms.

Oh, and secondly, did I mention that tent pegs make for a great defensive weapon?

The Tent Peg Strategy offers a vision of feminine strength and greatness. Inspired by women like Jael in Judges 4–5, it equips women with the principles they need to live faithfully in their day-to-day lives.

We meet Jael in a moment of political upheaval: Israel is at war with the Canaanites, and God's people are oppressed under Sisera's iron chariots. Her husband, Heber, chose political safety over covenant loyalty, allying with Canaan's king. Yet when Sisera, fleeing the battlefield, stumbled toward their tent, it was Jael—not Heber—who acted with courage, foresight, and faithfulness.

Rooted in her home yet engaged in the political moment, Jael was no bystander. When Sisera collapsed in her tent, she reached not for a sword but for what she knew best: the tent peg and mallet she had used countless times to anchor her home against desert winds. With one steady blow, she drove the tent peg through Sisera's skull and defeated God's enemy—just as Deborah had prophesied. And, in the next chapter, Deborah praises Jael as "the most blessed among women." A blessing, it turns out, that only appears one other time in the Bible, when Elizabeth praises Mary, the mother of God.

Of course, I doubt most of us will find ourselves in the same situation. Jael's story is descriptive (telling us how God worked through her) but certainly not prescriptive (telling us exactly how we should act toward enemies).

As one blog summarized a Charles Spurgeon sermon on sin, "We should not be content," he warned, "to see our sins merely fleeing from us; we should pursue them and drive them into the ground—dead—with a nail."[25] Indeed, as Christians today, we do not fight "against flesh and blood, but against the rulers, against the authorities, against the cosmic powers over this present darkness, against the spiritual forces of evil in the heavenly places" (Ephesians 6:12).

Jael was not violent for violence's sake. She did not go into battle, nor seek glory or vengeance. She acted when the fight came to her door, crushing the head of Israel's enemy the way Christ, the true Cornerstone, would one day crush Satan's head on the cross. Indeed, as Zechariah prophesies in 10:4, "From him [God] shall come the cornerstone, from him the tent peg, from him the battle bow, from him every ruler—all of them together." This verse underscores that all true strength, authority, and deliverance flow from God alone, showing that Jael's victory was not hers by might, but a foreshadowing of the greater triumph secured in Christ. The same is true for us today.

Under Jesus Christ's New Covenant, this means that we are called to root out and put to death sin when it creeps near. This begins in our own lives and extends into our families, communities, and nation. Where the Bible calls Christians to be peacemakers, many have settled for peace-*fakers* by lacking the courage or clarity to oppose sin or wrongdoing. Like Jael with the tent peg and mallet, God has already equipped you with the skills you need to defeat sin when it comes knocking at your door.

Mother, Maiden, Matriarch

The Tent Peg Strategy also follows a biblical pattern of growth and maturity. In his "Introduction to Biblical Theology" paper, James B. Jordan describes the male journey of discipleship through the roles of priest, king, and prophet.[26] The priest obeys God's law. The king internalizes that law, applies it with wisdom, and rules well. Finally, the prophet, having walked with God for years, speaks with authority, intercedes for others, and counsels nations.

While Jordan applies this to men, the framework finds a natural parallel in women's lives. The priest stage corresponds with the maiden, learning obedience and faithfulness to God's Word. The king stage parallels the mother, exercising wisdom, stewardship, and leadership within the home and community. Finally, the prophet stage aligns with the matriarch, the woman whose wisdom and counsel shape families, churches, and even nations.

Jordan notes that maturity is not about abandoning earlier stages but building upon them. "You don't cease to be a priest when you become a king. . . . Similarly, you don't cease to be a priest and king when you become a prophet. You still obey the law, still rule with wisdom, even as you now advise others and help shape what comes next."[27]

Importantly, these stages do not always follow age or circumstance. A woman could be ninety and still be a maiden spiritually if she has not cultivated wisdom or courage. Another might be young yet walk with the maturity of a mother because she has been tested by life, rooted herself in God's Word, and learned to live faithfully.

The chapters of this book follow the same trajectory. We begin with the maiden, exploring the importance of discernment, shrewdness, resourcefulness, and hospitality. Then we move to the mother stage and explore women who work alongside their husbands in a shared mission and disciple the next generation. Finally, we arrive at the matriarch and see women like Deborah, Abigail, and Sarah, whose lives anchor families, guide communities, and speak on behalf of God as they counsel and negotiate. While girl-boss feminism preaches a gospel of "progress," this movement does not necessarily mean that the girl boss is growing in maturity. Like Paul warns, she is often "always learning and never able to arrive at a knowledge of the truth" (2 Timothy 3:7). Instead of clinging on for dear life to the "maiden status," this book explores something far more meaningful and life-giving: what it looks like to walk closer to the Lord in faithful stewardship of all *He* has given *you*.

Whether you are a student preparing for the future, a single woman investing in your church and community, a mother raising young children, or an older woman guiding the next generation, your season matters. Your faithfulness matters.

Some readers grew up with blurred lines between men and women, where boys and girls were given the same life script for career, family, and calling. Others were raised with a healthy vision for home and family but want to understand its biblical foundations more clearly. Still others long for marriage and children but find themselves waiting and wondering how to live with wisdom right now.

Wherever you are, this book invites you to recover a biblical vision of womanhood rooted in faithfulness to Christ above all. The Tent Peg Strategy is not another internet trend or ideology. It is a call to courage, clarity, and maturity for every season of a woman's life. "The wisest of women builds her house, but folly with her own hands tears it down" (Proverbs 14:1). Like Jael, you already hold the tools in your hands. My prayer is that this book helps you use them for the glory of God and the good of the world.

PRINCIPLE ONE

Discernment

So when the woman saw that the tree was good for food, and that it was a delight to the eyes, and that the tree was to be desired to make one wise, she took of its fruit and ate, and she also gave some to her husband who was with her, and he ate. Then the eyes of both were opened, and they knew that they were naked. And they sewed fig leaves together and made themselves loincloths.

—Genesis 3:6–7

Growing up in the pine-shadowed backroads of rural South Georgia, the line between nature and the home was, at times, more of a suggestion than a boundary. Despite every screened door and sealed crack, the outside world still found its way in. Birds sometimes darted through open doors. Owls, having entered unnoticed during a period of construction, took up residence in our attic. Mice and other small creatures were regular, if unwelcome, visitors. But nothing ever quite unnerved me like snakes.

In my childhood, serpents didn't just slither in folklore; they slithered in our vents, our drawers, and in our dreams. I remember one afternoon at my grandmother's house. As we sat chatting in the living room, a snake silently uncoiled from a ceiling vent, descending above our heads like a scene from a thriller. Another time, I stepped on a black snake barefoot while walking across our yard. And then there's the story my mother tells from her newlywed days, back when she and my father were still renovating their house. She opened a bathroom drawer and found a snake curled up inside. She screamed, but my father, characteristically calm, took care of it without blinking.

The most unforgettable encounter, though, was both terrifying and—if I'm honest—a little funny. I was in elementary school, riding the golf cart with my sister and a few friends at my grandmother's house. As we sped down the hill, a rattlesnake lunged at us mere feet from the golf cart. We raced, wide-eyed, to tell our grandmother. Recognizing the danger, she didn't hesitate. She grabbed a gun in one hand and a shovel in the other. What happened next lives in my memory as something between legend and reality: with a steady stride, she approached the snake, shot it, and then severed its head with the shovel. Grandma: 1; Snake: 0.

Perhaps because of these experiences, I had a recurring nightmare for many years. In it, I was trapped, unable to escape from our yard or my grandmother's, and surrounded by snakes. There was no safe step forward, only the paralyzing sight of snakes slithering all around me.

Looking back, I can see that those experiences and dreams mirrored a deeper truth: dangerous and deceptive influences can creep into our homes, threatening the very place that's meant to be safe and peaceful.

It is no coincidence that in the Bible, gardens often represent the home as sacred, enclosed spaces of communion and cultivation. Nor is it accidental that the serpent's first attack was not in the wilderness, but in the Garden of Eden itself. From the very beginning, the enemy has always targeted the home.

The serpent's attack was in and against the home where we raise our children, love our spouses, build community, and walk with God. And just like in the literal gardens of my childhood, serpents still sneak in. But these days, they are not always covered in scales.

Some serpents come disguised in half-truths and whispered lies. They slither into conversations as gossip, into pulpits as distorted doctrine, and into relationships as manipulation or betrayal. Just as my grandmother didn't hesitate to confront the threat in her yard, so we must be ready to confront the spiritual threats that creep into our homes and lives. These attacks of the serpent target our very souls, aiming to sink deadly venom into our hearts and minds.

Principle One: Discernment

This is why it is so important that Christian women begin with a serious cultivation of the first tent peg: discernment. It's the Spirit-led ability to see what is good, true, and worthy of praise, even when our emotions, circumstances, or culture don't. It's knowing the difference between pink and blue, truth and almost-truth, and life and death. True discernment keeps its eyes on Jesus and helps us do the right thing, in the right way, at the right time. Easier said than done, right?

Like the rudder on a ship, it gives us a true bearing so we can move toward what is right and away from what is destructive, harmful, or unwise. Without it, we drift. And the truth is, many people do drift, whether it is struggling to make the best decision about college, finances and budgeting, which job to take, where to attend church, and practically, what TV shows, music, and videos we consume. How many people have been led astray or blunted in their ability to hear the Holy Spirit after building a life of mindless consumption of reality TV, materialistic music, and smutty erotic books? Even seemingly "harmless" shows like *Schitt's Creek* or *Friends* have gone a long way in normalizing homosexuality, hook-up culture, cohabitation, and culture where the ultimate truth is whatever makes you happy. The greatest damage, like we see in the Garden of Eden, comes from those subtle distortions.

This is why discernment is the first principle. All the others—shrewdness, resourcefulness, hospitality, marriage, motherhood, and matriarchy—depend on it. Applied without discernment, each one can twist into something it was never meant to be. Shrewdness becomes an excuse for manipulation. Resourcefulness sacrifices children on the altar of ambition. Hospitality turns into performance or disappears under the glow of screens. Marriage erodes under self-fulfillment. Motherhood bends toward neglect or control. Matriarchy withers as women chase youthfulness instead of faithfulness.

The problem isn't the principles themselves. It's that, without discernment rooted in God's Word, they drift off course. They become *almost* right. And almost right can still wreck a home. As Proverbs 14:12 says, "There is a way that seems right to a man, but its end is the way to death." Discernment keeps that from happening. It tells us not just what could be done, but what should be done in a way that honors Christ. It keeps the tent standing when the winds blow.

This is why the first temptation in the Bible targeted discernment. The serpent did not begin by denying God outright. He started by twisting what God had said, taking what was clear and making it seem uncertain. It was not a bold attack on Eve's courage or devotion. It was a subtle attack that called into question the clarity of God's Word in favor of her own judgment.

Did God Really Say?

There's a reason that the story of Eve and the serpent, Satan, has been told again and again: this dynamic of deception is still playing out in our world today.

After God's majestic work in Genesis 1 and His intimate creation of Adam and Eve in Genesis 2, Genesis 3 begins with a sudden, unsettling shift: "Now the serpent was more crafty than any other beast of the field that the Lord God had made" (Genesis 3:1a) From the very first line, we're drawn into the garden's stillness, where the serpent slithers along the very path God Himself had walked with Adam and Eve. Adam was nearby, but the serpent deliberately singled out Eve, setting the stage for the first act of spiritual seduction.

Instead of coming at Eve with an obvious attack that would have put her on her guard, the serpent took a different approach. He didn't hiss or threaten. He didn't even look dangerous. He just asked a question: "Did God actually say?" (Genesis 3:1b). And in that one simple question, he planted a seed of doubt that became a crack in Eve's trust in God's goodness and His plan.

Deception rarely begins with an outright lie. It starts with distortion. The serpent capitalized on that subtle shift. He moved Eve's focus from all that God had *provided* to the one thing He had *prohibited*—eating of the tree of the knowledge of good and evil. The tone of the passage even mirrors this movement: while Genesis 2 and the first part of verse one in Genesis 3 uses "the Lord God" (*Yahweh-Elohim*), the personal, covenantal name of God, the serpent strips that name down to simply "God" (Elohim). This change makes God seem distant, abstract, and impersonal. Eve echoes that shift in her own language throughout their conversation, too.

The serpent doesn't come right out and say, "God is evil." He doesn't have to. He just questions God's motives. "'For God knows that when you eat of it your eyes will be opened, and you will be like God, knowing good and evil'" (3:5). The suggestion is clear: *God is holding out on you.* The implication? *If you want wisdom, if you want fullness, you'll have to take it for yourself.*

And so, Eve looked. She saw with the eyes of practicality that the fruit was "good for food," then with the eyes of desire that it was a "delight to the eyes," and finally with the eyes of ambition that it was "desirable to make one wise" (Genesis 3:6).

It's important to note that her decision was based on an external assessment that was pragmatic, aesthetic, and self-serving. The fruit made sense to her. It looked good. It felt right. And that, ultimately, is the root of deception: choosing what feels right over what God *says* is right.

So, Eve took the forbidden fruit, and she ate. And she gave some to Adam, who was standing there, too. The serpent didn't force her to disobey God. He just planted the thought and watched it grow.

Of course, God loves us too much to leave us how we are in the brokenness and chaos of sin. So even as God judged Eve and Adam, God also revealed His marvelous plan for redemption. Indeed, what the serpent meant for evil, God used for good. "I will put enmity between you and the woman, and between your offspring and her offspring; he shall bruise your head, and you shall bruise his heel" (Genesis 3:15). Moments after sin entered the world, God turned to the serpent with a message of hope and victory: God's own Son would be born as one of Eve's children, and He would crush the deceiver once and for all.

What happened in Eden was not just Eve's story. It's our story. The serpent still whispers. He still twists God's words, makes sin look reasonable, and uses half-truths to question God's goodness. He sows lies in our relationships, in what we watch and read, in the assumptions we carry about success, identity, marriage, and parenting. And just like Eve, we often make choices based on what feels practical, looks appealing, or seems wise in the moment, without really asking if it aligns with God's Word.

Lady Wisdom: Not *The 48 Laws of Power* but an Invitation to Know Christ

Eve's story shows us what happens when discernment fails. But the Bible doesn't leave us there. Instead, it offers us a faithful model: Lady Wisdom. Through her, we learn what it means not only to avoid deception, but to grow in godly wisdom. Lady Wisdom appears in Proverbs 1, 8, and 9 when wisdom speaks as a woman calling out in the streets, inviting people to follow her ways and find life. She is not a real person but a literary picture of God's wisdom at work in the world. As Christians, the Bible tells us to pay attention to her, learn from her, and let her lead us toward the kind of wisdom that ultimately points to life in Jesus Christ.

In a culture obsessed with influence, quick results, and self-optimization, it's no surprise that many women, even in the church, are tempted to approach wisdom the same way they approach success: through formulas, life hacks, or step-by-step strategies. Just read the right books (like this one!), listen to the right podcasts, implement a few spiritual disciplines, and voilà—*wisdom*.

It would be easy, and certainly tempting, to reduce Lady Wisdom to something like that: a neat listicle or spiritualized self-help guide. But the Bible doesn't describe Lady Wisdom as a Machiavellian life hack like Robert Greene's book *The 48 Laws of Power*, and it certainly doesn't fit into a one-size-fits-all checklist like "Six Steps to Becoming an Influential Matriarch," as is often promoted by the more performative corners of tradwife culture.

As a Type A overachiever, I've often wanted to add "get wisdom" to my to-do list. Yet wisdom doesn't come through striving; it grows out of seeking God above all else. The Bible personifies wisdom as a woman to show that it's relational at its core. To grow in wisdom is to grow in relationship with Jesus Christ, who embodies wisdom fully and perfectly. Through her, we learn that wisdom is not only about discernment or knowledge but about knowing God Himself.

Proverbs 1:7 tells us, "The fear of the Lord is the beginning of knowledge; fools despise wisdom and instruction," and Proverbs 9:10 echoes this truth: "The fear of the Lord is the beginning of wisdom, and the knowledge of the Holy One is insight." There is no secret formula. No hidden knowledge. There is only Jesus Christ, the incarnate Son of God, and a life shaped by knowing Him, loving what He loves, and walking in His ways. Just as wisdom in Proverbs reveals God's nature, Jesus reveals God's person. Wisdom gives voice to divine truth; Jesus embodies that truth in human form. "For God so loved the world, that he gave his only Son, that whoever believes in him should not perish but have eternal life" (John 3:16). Through Lady Wisdom we come to see what God is like, but through Jesus we come to know Him personally.

The Bible describes Lady Wisdom this way:

- She builds her house with care.
- She orders it, fills it with rich food and wine, mentors the young, and from this place of abundance, she invites the simple to dine with her.
- She nurtures, beautifies, and transforms the world by turning raw materials into meaningful, life-giving gifts.
- She was with God at creation, delighting in His work and rejoicing in the world He made.
- By her kings reign, rulers govern wisely, and enduring riches and honor are found in her ways.
- She judges rightly and offers salvation to those who follow her ways. Lady Wisdom never wields a sword, yet no battle is won without her.

This wisdom isn't reserved for the spiritual elite. James 1:5–8 makes it clear:

> If any of you lacks wisdom, let him ask God, who gives generously to all without reproach, and it will be given him. But let him ask in faith, with no doubting, for the one who doubts is like a wave of the sea that is driven and tossed by the wind. For that person must not suppose that he will receive anything from the Lord; he is a double-minded man, unstable in all his ways.

God isn't surprised by our need for wisdom. In fact, the Bible makes it clear that we don't just need a little advice here and there. No, we need *Him*. Desperately. And the good news is that He delights to give us Himself and His wisdom. James tells us to ask, believing that God is a good Father who loves to give good gifts to His children. And if your faith feels small, you can even ask the Spirit to help you trust that promise. God gives generously, without criticism or shame, to all who ask.

The Fourth "M": Madness, or the Way of Lady Folly

In the introduction, we explored the maiden, mother, and matriarch progression of a woman's life. These descriptions don't depend on a woman's marital status or whether she has children, but they do reflect where she is on her journey to becoming a wise and mature woman in the Lord. Maidens learn obedience to God's Word, mothers exercise leadership, and matriarchs offers life-giving counsel in the highest places. Yet there is another path, a counterfeit one, offered by the enemy. This is the way of madness.

This is the path personified in Lady Folly, the spiritual antithesis of Lady Wisdom. Where wisdom builds, folly dismantles. Where wisdom calls others toward life, folly seduces them toward death.

In Proverbs 9, the narrator introduces us to Lady Folly immediately after the majestic description of Lady Wisdom. The contrast is deliberate and sharp. While both women take a seat in the "high places" of the town and call out to the simple, their messages and motive could not be more opposed.

> The woman Folly is loud; she is seductive and knows nothing. She sits at the door of her house; she takes a seat on the highest places of the town, calling to those who pass by, who are going straight on their way, "Whoever is simple, let him turn in here!" And to him who lacks sense she says, "Stolen water is sweet, and bread eaten in secret is pleasant." But he does not know that the dead are there, that her guests are in the depths of Sheol. (Proverbs 9:13–18)

Lady Folly imitates Lady Wisdom by sitting in the high places and inviting guests to her table. But while Lady Wisdom offers rich wine and fine bread, Lady Folly has only water and stolen bread to give. It takes time, foresight, preparation, and technical skill to ferment wine and bake bread, and Lady Folly has none of these virtues.

This contrast isn't just symbolic. Scripture gives us real women who embody Lady Folly: Jezebel, who manipulated King Ahab through deceit and idolatry; Delilah, who betrayed Samson and God's people to the Philistines; and the adulterous woman in Proverbs 7, who lures men with flattering words and reckless passion, perhaps echoing Solomon's many foreign wives who led Israel into idolatry. These women were not ignorant victims of circumstance. They chose to reject the fear of the Lord and wield their influence for destruction rather than for good.

This dynamic is no less present today. Many influences on social media, in celebrity Christianity, and even within the church, *appear* wise. In an age of platforms and personal brands, we must be discerning. We should seek advice from real women whose lives and character we can see, beyond a curated sixty-second reel. Consider the online persona "Patriarchy Hannah," a so-called tradwife influencer who apparently fabricated stories about her dozen children, her supposedly perfect marriage, and her hyper-idealized life as a wife and mother. Thousands of women, comparing themselves to her impossible standards, felt inadequate and discouraged, only to later learn it was all a lie. Lady Folly still uses the same tools: deception, comparison, and the promise of secret pleasures or perfect lives that lead only to disappointment and death.

So how do we resist her call? How do we become women marked by wisdom rather than madness? In the following section, we'll look at practical steps for cultivating discernment, testing the voices we follow, and anchoring ourselves in the fear of the Lord.

The Tent Peg Strategy in Action

Godly discernment isn't a "get wise quick" plan, but we can take practical steps to grow in it. One of the clearest comes from the Apostle Paul, who warns against the kind of open-mindedness that keeps people from standing firm in God's truth.

> But understand this, that in the last days there will come times of difficulty. For people will be lovers of self, lovers of money, proud, arrogant, abusive, disobedient to their parents, ungrateful, unholy, heartless, unappeasable, slanderous, without self-control, brutal, not loving good, treacherous, reckless, swollen with conceit, lovers of pleasure rather than lovers of God, having the appearance of godliness, but denying its

> power. Avoid such people. *For among them are those who creep into households and capture weak women, burdened with sins and led astray by various passions, always learning and never able to arrive at a knowledge of the truth.* (2 Timothy 3:1–7, my emphasis added)

That description sounds like today's headlines. Every vice on Paul's list works against godly discernment. They train us to trust our own wisdom instead of God's. As we saw illustrated in Genesis 3, Paul warns Timothy about people who "creep into households and capture weak women." How do they do it? By appealing to emotions, stirring up distracting passions, and repeating the same old lie that knowledge apart from God brings freedom. That lie deceived Eve, and it still deceives today. Discernment is not optional. It is the difference between a home protected by truth and a home overtaken by lies.

Paul also warns about those who are "always learning and never able to arrive at a knowledge of the truth." Lifelong learning is good, but Paul is describing people who refuse to submit to what the Bible clearly teaches. For example, the Bible speaks plainly about sexuality (Romans 1:26–27), the covenant of marriage between one man and one woman (Genesis 2:24; Matthew 19:4–6), and the call to holiness in every part of life (1 Peter 1:15–16). Yet some treat cultural trends or personal experiences as equal to or greater than God's Word. They appear wise and open-minded, but Paul says they never reach the truth. We must avoid becoming people who look godly but reject the power of the gospel to transform us.

This is why Jesus calls us to be innocent as doves and wise as serpents. Failing to stand on God's Word opens the door to deception. It teaches us to love what is evil and follow the world's wisdom instead of God's.

We all know how our own hearts can deceive us. Thoughts creep in: *Everyone does it. It's just this once. It's not that big of a deal. Surely God doesn't care about this one decision.* We chase what looks appealing, such as wealth, success, intelligence, beauty, or social status. We tell ourselves that if something promises happiness, it must be good. But the Bible warns us that appearances can be misleading.

Here are five areas where women especially need discernment today:

1. Careerism Above All Else

Kaitlyn was the woman everyone admired. Stunningly beautiful, a primetime TV personality, and a policy director at the top of her field. Yes, she was the picture of "having it all." Marriage and children, she thought, could wait. But when she hit thirty-eight, she read a simple blog post about the joys of marriage and motherhood stopped her in her tracks. "It was like God pulled back the curtain," she told me. "I realized I had built this glittering life, but none of it could give me the things I actually wanted most." She married her longtime boyfriend that year and had two children by forty-two, but she often speaks with sobering honesty about the years she can never get back.

"My career was soaring," Kaitlyn said, "but my real life, the one with a husband and children, was still sitting on the runway. And no one warned me I might run out of time." Now, at the height of her career, she describes this ongoing tension between her work life *imbalance*. Stepping back as director, or moving part-time, would allow her more time with her children, but it would mean letting go of the career she had worked so hard to get. Yet staying on that path meant missing the moments with her children she had longed for and now deeply values.

Kaitlyn's story is a warning for our generation. Career aspirations are not inherently bad. Work matters. But when career consumes us, such that we build our marriage, children, Sabbath rest, and spiritual growth around our jobs, we believe the old lie that fulfillment can be built apart from faithfulness to God's good design for the family.

Rachel Campos-Duffy's story offers another perspective. She and her husband, Secretary of Transportation Sean Duffy, chose to prioritize marriage and children early, even as her television career was taking off. Rather than try to do it all at one time, she stepped back from her own career to raise their children and support her husband. Today, as a mother of nine with a thriving media career, she is a powerful example of how careers can stretch across decades. By investing in her family first, she built the foundation for a longer career that did not come at the cost of her home.

2. *Inundated with Information and AI Answers*

Lindsey thought she was staying informed. As she described it to me, she started her mornings scrolling news feeds, listening to podcasts at lunch, and following dozens of "experts" on Instagram. "I thought I was wise," she admitted to me, "but honestly, I was just anxious and exhausted. The more information I consumed, the less peace I had."

Her turning point came when her ten-year-old daughter said, "Mom, you're always looking at your phone." That simple observation hit hard. Lindsey realized her constant intake was shaping her more than God's Word ever did. "I had to delete apps, set boundaries, and remember that wisdom doesn't come from the algorithm," she said. "It comes from God."

Discernment in the digital age means recognizing that constant access to information does not make us wiser. It requires setting limits so we can hear God's voice above the noise. Sometimes the most spiritual thing you can do is turn off the phone, open your Bible, and give your full attention to the people in front of you.

When I spoke with Anna, she described a similar wake-up call. She used to love reading her Bible early in the morning. But slowly, her routine shifted. Instead of Scripture, she opened her laptop. She started asking chatbots about marriage, parenting, and even theology. "It felt easier," she admitted. "Why search the Bible when ChatGPT could give me an instant answer?"

But the more Anna relied on quick answers, the less she thought for herself and the less she prayed. The chatbot seemed helpful, even spiritual at times, but it slowly replaced her own study of God's Word. "I didn't even notice it happening," she said. "I let convenience train me not to think deeply about anything."

Canadian philosopher Marshall McLuhan famously said, "the medium is the message." His point was that technology must be judged not only by what it does but by how it reshapes the way we live and think. He used the railway as an example: trains didn't invent movement or roads, but they radically changed the *pace* and *pattern* of human life, creating entirely new kinds of cities, jobs, and relationships.[1]

In the same way, constant access to information, whether through social media or AI, doesn't just "keep us informed." It changes the way we think about wisdom itself. It trains us to expect instant answers instead of deep reflection, convenience instead of prayerful study, and quick summaries instead of real understanding. McLuhan warned that the content blinds us to the real effect: the technology itself is shaping the scale and form of our lives. That is why discernment means asking not only, "What am I learning?" but also, "How is this technology shaping the way I learn, the way I pray, and the way I hear from God?"

3. Sexual Sin and the War on the Body

Emily grew up in church but slowly absorbed what the culture said about sex—that it was private, personal, and no one else's concern. When she and her boyfriend moved in together, it felt like the practical next step. "We just thought it made sense," she said. "We wanted to see if we were compatible before making it official." But looking back, Emily admitted it didn't work the way she hoped. "I thought living together would protect me from getting hurt. Instead, it chipped away at my faith and left me feeling less secure, not more."

Emily's story isn't unique. Many couples don't make a deliberate decision to live together; they simply slide into it because it seems easier. For some couples, it means less driving back and forth, fewer boundaries, or fewer conversations about commitment.

But the research is sobering. The Institute for Family Studies reports that couples who cohabit before marriage have lower levels of trust, higher rates of divorce, and are less satisfied in their marriages overall. David Ayers, a professor at Grove City College, has also shown how common cohabitation has become even among evangelicals, despite these clear warnings. Part of the problem is what cohabitation teaches: if marriage begins with the idea that you can leave whenever you want, it shapes expectations about commitment from the start.[2]

Our culture calls sexual "freedom" empowerment, but in practice, it often leads to confusion, broken trust, and deep regret. The Bible tells a better story. God's design for sex and marriage is not about withholding joy but about guarding it. In the Bible, the Apostle Paul warns, "Flee from sexual immorality . . . but the sexually immoral person sins against his own body" (1 Corinthians 6:18). Yet it's common to hear conservatives condemn the sexual sins of others while justifying premarital sex or living together before marriage in their own lives. Even among evangelicals, this is an area of self-deception that we must recognize and reject.

4. Toxic Empathy

Rachel wanted to be kind. When her friend came out as transgender, she felt torn between biblical truth and her desire to keep the friendship. "So I used the pronouns," she admitted. "I told myself it was just being compassionate. But then I realized I was discipling my own kids to stay silent when the culture demands their approval."

Rachel's story isn't unique. Many Christians wrestle with the same tension of wanting to show compassion yet fearing that speaking truth will be seen as "too political." This is exactly what evangelical author and podcaster Allie Beth Stuckey warns about in *Toxic Empathy: How Progressives Exploit Christian Compassion* when she writes, "The erroneous conflation of love and empathy has convinced the masses that to be loving, we must feel the same way they do. . . . Toxic empathy says we must not only share their feelings, but affirm their feelings and choices as valid, justified, and good."[3]

That confusion extends beyond personal relationships. It now shapes public policy, where "compassion" often drives decisions that leave the innocent unprotected. My friend Maria saw this firsthand in Charlotte, North Carolina, where prosecutors and lawmakers insisted that locking up repeat offenders was "unjust." In reality, these "soft-on-crime" laws cleared the way for tragedy.

Take for example the heartbreaking murder of Iryna Zarutska, a twenty-three-year-old Ukrainian refugee. In August 2025, she was stabbed to death by a man who had been arrested fourteen times over the last twenty years for altercations including armed robbery, a schizophrenia diagnosis, and repeatedly displaying violent behavior. A criminal justice system that fails to take crime seriously leaves the vulnerable exposed and the dangerous unrestrained. It says that lives like Iryna's aren't worth protecting.

This is what happens when, as Allie Beth Stuckey writes, "feelings are often misaligned with reality and can actually blind us from—rather than lead us to—wisdom."[4]

5. Soft Christianity and the Third Way

In many churches today, sermons sound like TED Talks. Sin is rebranded as "brokenness," judgment is avoided, and pastors pride themselves on being winsome while the culture burns. This "Third Way" Christianity claims to rise above politics but usually just echoes the world's talking points with Bible verses sprinkled in.

One mom told me, "I realized my kids had heard more about climate activism and social justice in Sunday School than about sin, holiness, or the gospel itself." She isn't alone. This is the fruit of Third Way Christianity: a generation hesitant to offend anyone and unsure how to defend anything.

And then came the assassination of Charlie Kirk, founder and president of Turning Point USA, in September 2025. His death exposed the emptiness of "winsome" Christianity, the myth of a morally neutral public square, and the fantasy that seeker-sensitive sermons would somehow transform the world. When a man dies for speaking the truth, it forces the church to face a question it has long avoided: if the gospel costs this much, why are so many pastors bending over backward to make it palatable?

As evangelist Jim Wilson once said, "Soft words make hard hearts. Hard words make soft hearts."[5] As Christians, we must tell the truth, even when the truth offends, because only the truth can save. Indeed, "Faithful are the wounds of a friend; profuse are the kisses of an enemy" (Proverbs 27:6).

The Tent Peg Strategy: A Step-by-Step Guide for Practicing Godly Discernment

1. Begin with the Fear of the Lord

Start every day by acknowledging God's authority over your life. And especially before you rush into decisions or conversations, pause and pray, "Lord, help me see this through Your eyes, not my own." I've seen women begin their mornings this way, and it changes the whole tone of their day. Indeed, they speak differently, they parent differently, and they make choices with eternity in view because they've started with humble submission to God's Word.

2. Saturate Your Mind with Scripture

You can't recognize truth if you don't know what truth sounds like. As Romans 12:2 says, "Do not be conformed to this world, but be transformed by the renewal of your mind, that by testing you may discern what is the will of God, what is good and acceptable and perfect." That means opening your Bible every day, even if it's just one chapter. Write down one thing you learn about God's character or His commandments, and when decisions come up, ask, "What has God already said about this?" I remember a friend who was deciding whether to take a high-paying job that would require her to travel often on Sundays. Reading what the Ten Commandments had to say about Sabbath rest and the book of Proverbs reminded her that greed leads to trouble, and she realized her motives weren't pure. The Bible has a way of cutting through the fog like that. Of course, it would also be incomplete to fall into a "just me and Jesus" mindset apart from a vibrant Bible-believing Church where we can hear the Word exegetically preached, taught, and applied to our lives.

3. Pray for Wisdom—and Expect It

Before you make decisions, stop and ask God for wisdom. James 1:5 teaches us that "If any of you lacks wisdom, let him ask God, who gives generously to all without reproach, and it will be given him." God freely gives us His wisdom if we ask with faith.

4. Slow Down and Test Everything

The world tells you to trust your gut and act fast. God's Word tells us to "test everything; hold fast what is good. Abstain from every form of evil" (1 Thessalonians 5:21–22). Before jumping into a decision, ask: Does this align with the Bible? Will this honor Christ? Will this bear good fruit a year from now, or does it just look appealing right now? Eve looked at the fruit and thought it looked good, but discernment means digging beneath the surface.

5. Seek Godly Counsel

Wise people ask other wise people for input. Proverbs 11:14 reminds us that "Where there is no guidance, a people falls, but in an abundance of counselors there is safety." So look for women who love God's Word and whose lives show it. I once asked advice from two older moms before making a major parenting decision, and their stories kept me from repeating mistakes they had made. Good counsel helps you see blind spots you didn't even know were there.

6. Watch for Counterfeits

Not everything that sounds good is from God. Indeed, "even Satan disguises himself as an angel of light" (2 Corinthians 11:14), so pay attention to the *fruit*. True wisdom leads to peace, holiness, and obedience; false wisdom leads to compromise, chaos, and sin. A college student I knew once joined a group that talked about "love" constantly, but the group denied core truths about Jesus. It looked good on the surface but was rotten underneath. Discernment helps you spot the serpent's lies wrapped in spiritual language.

7. Examine the Desires of Your Heart

Our hearts can trick us, and the truth is that we are often our own best salespersons. When we want something badly enough, we can rationalize almost anything by twisting circumstances, ignoring red flags, or even convincing ourselves that because it is an option, then it *must* be from God. But Jeremiah 17:9 warns us that "The heart is deceitful above all things, and desperately sick; who can understand it?" I've prayed Psalm 139:23–24 many times, asking: "Search me, O God . . . and lead me in the way everlasting!" One friend admitted to me that she stayed in a relationship too long because she wanted the attention and security it offered. But when she was honest about her motives, she knew that her own faith was growing weaker the longer she dated this unbeliever.

8. Obey Quickly Once You Know

Discernment isn't complete until you act on what God shows you. James 1:22 warns us not to just hear the Word but to do it. I knew a couple who had been living together for years before coming to faith in Jesus Christ. As they read the Bible, it became clear that God calls for sexual purity before marriage. They didn't wait to obey until it was convenient or until family members approved. Instead, they separated for a time, got counseling, and were married a few months later. It wasn't easy, but they said the peace and joy that followed their obedience was worth every hard step. Wisdom isn't proven by what we know; it's proven by what we do.

9. Keep a Journal of God's Faithfulness

Write down how God has guided you, provided for you, and corrected you in the past. When new decisions come, go back and read those stories. Remembering God's faithfulness builds confidence for the future because wisdom begins when we realize how short life is and how much we need His guidance every single day. As Psalm 90:12 says, "So teach us to number our days that we may get a heart of wisdom." The real danger comes when we forget God's promises, His past provision, or the lessons learned in our own failures. The moment we forget God's character and faithfulness, we start believing we can manage life on our own terms.

10. Learn to Hear the Holy Spirit

Discernment isn't just an intellectual exercise. God made us whole beings with minds, bodies, emotions, and spirits such that learning to recognize His voice often involves paying attention to all four. Hebrews 5:14 says, "But solid food is for the mature, for those who have their powers of discernment trained by constant practice to distinguish good from evil."

Here's what this looks like: When you're facing a decision, pause and notice what's happening inside you. How does your body respond? Do you feel tense, restless, light-headed, or at peace? What emotions surface? Do you feel joy, dread, excitement, anxiety? Then test those feelings with God's Word and prayer.

Over time, you may begin to recognize patterns. I remember once being offered a speaking opportunity that seemed perfect on paper. But every time I prayed, my chest felt heavy, my thoughts raced, and peace was nowhere to be found. It turns out, I was anxious about finding childcare and felt like it would be too difficult on Jack and the girls to travel at that time. So, I said no. It was too much on our schedule at that time.

The Holy Spirit never contradicts God's Word, but He often uses conviction, unease, or deep peace to guide us. The more you practice listening with your whole self—mind renewed by Scripture, emotions surrendered to Christ, and taking time to listen to your body—the more quickly you'll recognize His voice leading you toward wisdom and obedience.

Conclusion

It can seem at first that God put the tree of the knowledge of good and evil in the Garden as a cruel test. But the tree was never meant to be an eternal "no." It was a "not yet." Adam and Eve were created innocent, like beloved children, learning day by day under the care of their Father. In time, as they grew in trust and obedience, I think God would have given them the very wisdom they tried to seize too soon. The Tree of the Knowledge of Good and Evil was not inherently evil. Adam and Eve's desire for wisdom and to be like God came *from God*. But to grasp for its fruit apart from God's timing was to disobey God's Word and reject the slow, sanctifying path of maturity He had designed for them. But what they lost in Eden, Christ restored in the New Covenant.

The Bible shows us a better way. Lady Wisdom calls out in the streets, inviting all who will listen to come and learn. She promises life, understanding, and honor to those who fear the Lord and walk in His ways. Through Christ, the Holy Spirit now forms us over time, teaching us to discern good from evil as we walk in obedience and grow into the maturity God always intended. The fruit they grabbed at the serpent's urging is now given in its proper season by the Father's hand, shaping us not into gods, but into children who bear His likeness in wisdom, holiness, and love.

PRINCIPLE TWO

Shrewdness

Then the LORD *God said to the woman, "What is this that you have done?" The woman said, "The serpent deceived me, and I ate." The* LORD *God said to the serpent, "Because you have done this, cursed are you above all livestock and above all beasts of the field; on your belly you shall go, and dust you shall eat all the days of your life. I will put enmity between you and the woman, and between your offspring and her offspring; he shall bruise your head, and you shall bruise his heel."*

—Genesis 3:13–15

At the turn of the twentieth century, a slight Irish missionary named Amy Carmichael walked the sun-scorched streets of southern India dressed as no Western woman was expected to dress. Wrapped in a sari, her skin darkened with coffee stains, she moved through temple courtyards where foreign eyes were not welcome. She had come to India to preach Christ, but what she encountered there would demand more than words. It would require shrewdness: a Spirit-led creativity to protect the vulnerable and advance the kingdom of God.

As she settled into life in India, Amy began hearing whispers about young girls called *devadasis*, children given to Hindu temples. Families, burdened by poverty or bound by vows, handed over their daughters as gifts to the gods. The reality was far darker. These girls were bound to ritual service, many forced into lives of prostitution. As Elisabeth Elliot describes it in her biography of Amy Carmichael, "Sometimes the Band had seen little girls, bought as infants from their mothers and reared in the temple-women's house where, by precept and example, they learned the 'trade.'"[1]

Their stories were whispered in villages, but when a frightened child named Preena appeared on Amy's doorstep in 1901, the rumors became flesh and blood. Preena had fled the temple where she was enslaved, her hands scarred by hot irons from an earlier attempt to escape. Clinging to Amy, she embraced her as her own mother. Amy later wrote, "The child told us things that darkened the sunlight. It was impossible to forget those things."[2] Against threats from temple priests and the looming risk of legal charges, Amy sheltered Preena. This act became the turning point of her life's work.

Rescuing one child quickly led to another. Soon Amy and her small band of coworkers found themselves devising ways to move children quietly and safely. "Wherever we went after that day we were constrained to gather facts about what appeared a great secret traffic in the souls and bodies of young children, and we searched for some way to save them, and could find no way. The helpless little things seemed to slip between our fingers as we stretched out our hands to grasp them."[3] Her methods were unconventional, sometimes dangerous, but always directed toward protecting the children entrusted to her.

As the rescues multiplied, Amy turned to the courts with equal resourcefulness. Temple authorities brought charges of kidnapping against her and demanded the return of children. Amy was careful to work within the Indian legal system, and when news of a child soon to be sold to the temple reached her, she had to act quickly to persuade the parents. When faced with the chance to redeem a little girl's freedom for one hundred rupees, she later shared in her book *Gold Cord*, "It was such an unheard-of thing to pay money for the redemption of a child."[4] Yet, as she and her Indian sisters prayed, an unexpected gift of that exact amount arrived. "We laid the cheque on the floor like a little new Gideon's fleece, and, kneeling round it, we thanked our heavenly Father."[5] By combining discretion, legal savvy, and unwavering faith, Amy carved out a safe haven where hundreds of boys and girls could grow in Christ.

What began as a hidden and responsive effort became a movement that helped expose and challenge an entire cultural system. Amy's life showed the fruit of faithful shrewdness to protect life and advance God's justice—first in the unexpected rescue of one child, then in an orphanage that became home to thousands, and eventually in laws that restricted the *devadasis* practice itself. What started as the risky courage of a single missionary soon bore national impact. Yet through threats, legal charges, and pressure from temple authorities, Amy never wavered in her calling to "bring good news to the poor . . . to bind up the brokenhearted, to proclaim liberty to the captives, and the opening of the prison to those who are bound" (Isaiah 61:1).

Throughout Amy Carmichael's life, she moved from an unknown and solitary actor willing to risk her life for young women fleeing temple prostitution, to a well-known leader of a movement that sparked lasting political change. She did not allow man's customs, when they clearly contradicted God's law, to dictate her actions. Amy feared God more than man. She used wisdom, courage, and shrewdness to protect children, and her faithfulness eventually brought hundreds to Jesus Christ.

The Tent Peg Strategy: Three Pathways of Biblical Shrewdness

Amy Carmichael's story stands in line with many faithful women before her who practiced shrewdness to protect life and uphold God's covenant promises. We, too, live in a world that demands such wisdom. As Aaron Renn, author of *Life in the Negative World: Confronting Challenges in an Anti-Christian Culture*, observes, our cultural moment is in a "negative world," where Christian beliefs no longer carry social benefits or equal respect.[6] Instead, biblical convictions are viewed with suspicion, hostility, or outright legal opposition. To live openly as Christians now means navigating a climate where truth is distorted and righteousness is branded as intolerance.

In this environment, shrewdness is an essential tent peg for today's women of faith. Biblical shrewdness is courageous wisdom applied with love to protect life, confront evil, and advance God's promises. Such shrewdness does not include manipulation or deception for selfish gain, and it adheres wholly to the Word of God to dictate what is good, lovely, and worthy of praise. Jesus Himself told His disciples to be "wise as serpents and innocent as doves" (Matthew 10:16), urging them to be prudent, strategic, and love God's Word above all else.

The Bible gives us a gallery of women who embodied this principle. The Egyptian midwives defied Pharaoh's decree with righteous deception, sparing the lives of Hebrew babies. Miriam's quick thinking preserved Moses's life and kept him close to his family. Rahab hid Israel's spies and chose allegiance to the living God over loyalty to her king. Tamar used a disguise to hold Judah accountable, and Rebekah acted decisively to protect God's covenantal line from going to a son who despised God's law. Each story shows women who, when pressed to the edge, acted with both courage and shrewdness in service of God's promises.

These examples, which we will explore in more depth, do not always provide step-by-step instructions for us to apply to our own lives, but they reveal a consistent truth: God blesses shrewd faithfulness. These women who acted with strategic wisdom were blessed with families, protection, or even a place in the lineage of Christ Himself. Their stories remind us that in times of danger, when the stakes are high and the choices are costly, godly shrewdness is one of God's good gifts to His people.

In the same way, the women of Scripture employ shrewdness most commonly in three ways:

1. They exercise shrewd judgment, prudence in public affairs, and careful preparation in home management.
2. They use shrewd means to protect life and uphold God's covenant promises.
3. They act shrewdly to expose wrong and bring about repentance, especially when they lack power or social standing.

1. Shrewdness in Judgment and Preparation

The Bible introduces us to two rival women in the book of Proverbs—Lady Wisdom and Lady Folly. Both are described as shrewd, both call out to the simple, and both seek to shape the lives of those who hear their voice. Yet their ends could not be more different. Lady Wisdom "dwell[s] with prudence" (Proverbs 8:12), and her words are rooted in righteousness and truth. She plans ahead, discerns the character of others, and directs her hearers toward life. Lady Folly, by contrast, is loud and seductive. She too is cunning, but her path leads to death. This contrast takes us back to Genesis 3, where the serpent's craftiness was bent toward destruction, twisting God's word and luring Eve into sin. The issue is not whether a woman will be shrewd, but whether her shrewdness will be guided by the fear of the Lord or by self-serving desire.

Scripture holds up the Proverbs 31 woman as a picture of shrewdness rightly applied. She buys a field and plants a vineyard, showing foresight in business. She clothes her household in scarlet, anticipating the winter ahead. She opens her mouth with wisdom with kind words on her tongue, and she manages her home with diligence and skill. None of these actions are dramatic or public like Rahab's misdirection or Miriam's intervention, yet they require constant discernment and careful preparation. They remind us that shrewdness is essential for the daily decisions of household management, extracurricular activity decisions, education, and financial investments to protect the home from hardship and loss.

This same kind of wisdom is needed in our homes today, especially in financial stewardship. For centuries, women had little direct authority over credit or banking, but today most women oversee or heavily influence their household budget. It wasn't until the 1970s that women first gained independent access to credit cards, and personal debt has risen sharply across the United States.[7] Such debt and consumerism have become normalized, often through unchecked spending habits that prioritize individual desires over family stability. While the connection is complex, the lesson remains: without shrewd discernment and foresight, households crumble under the weight of financial strain.

Jesus's parable of the minas (Luke 19:11–27) presses this home. The master entrusted ten servants with different amounts of money. Two invested wisely and doubled their allotment. One, afraid of risk, buried his coin in the ground. When the master returned, the fearful and unproductive servant was condemned because he failed to use his resources with shrewd courage. In the same way, women today are called to steward their resources with foresight and strategy.

2. *Shrewdness in Protecting Life and God's Covenant*

The opening of Exodus paints a chilling scene. Pharaoh, fearful of Israel's growing strength, commanded the death of every Hebrew boy at birth. His order fell to midwives—women entrusted with bringing life into the world—to carry it out, since they would be present at the births themselves. Two of them, Shiphrah and Puah, are remembered by name because they refused to obey. They feared God more than Pharaoh, and their holy defiance preserved countless infants. When confronted, they gave Pharaoh an answer that was clever and disarming: "'Because the Hebrew women are not like the Egyptian women, for they are vigorous and give birth before the midwife comes to them'" (Exodus 1:19). With this response, they protected life while avoiding direct confrontation with the king. By using words sparingly, disguising resistance in an explanation that was hard to challenge, and doing what was within their power to frustrate evil, they embodied shrewd faithfulness. The Bible says that because of their actions, God honored them by giving them families of their own. Their names endure as memorials of wisdom and courage, while Pharaoh's name in that passage is not even mentioned.

Moses's family soon demonstrated the same kind of discerning boldness. His mother, defying Pharaoh's order, hid him for three months. When concealment became impossible, she wove a basket, sealed it with tar, and set it afloat on the Nile with Moses inside. Whether they had any hope of salvation or simply couldn't bring themselves to see Moses killed by soldiers, the text doesn't say. In either case, Miriam, Moses's sister, stood watch. And, in the same way God would later part the Red Sea, God used the river as the means of His salvation for Moses.

When Pharaoh's daughter opened the basket and saw the crying child, her heart softened. At that moment, Miriam stepped forward with remarkable composure: "'Shall I go and call you a nurse from the Hebrew women to nurse the child for you?'" (Exodus 2:7). Miriam spoke no falsehood, but she also didn't reveal more than necessary. In that moment, God returned Moses to his own mother through Pharaoh's daughter and provided wages for his care. Miriam's shrewd offer was met with God's kindness in preserving Moses's life and gifting his mother with more time to care for him.

Many years later, Israel's journey brought them to the fortified city of Jericho. And here, on the very edge of the Promised Land, God chose to highlight another woman whose actions would shape salvation history. Though once a pagan prostitute, Rahab of Jericho stands as a striking example because she allied herself with Israel's God.

When Israelite spies entered her home, she hid the spies under stalks of flax on her roof and distracted the king's men with a swift misdirection: "'True, the men came to me, but I did not know where they were from. And when the gate was about to be closed at dark, the men went out. I do not know where the men went. Pursue them quickly, for you will overtake them'" (Joshua 2:4–5). Her words protected God's people and declared her faith in God's salvation: "for the Lord your God, he is God in the heavens above and on the earth beneath" (Joshua 2:11b). In return, she asked for mercy, and the scarlet cord in her window became the sign of salvation for her household. When Jericho fell, Rahab and her family were spared, and her name was written into the genealogy of Christ.

From the midwives and Miriam to Rahab, a clear pattern emerges. Each woman showed courage and wisdom in the face of great personal danger by protecting the innocent, speaking carefully, and trusting God to work through them. For Christian women today, this same wisdom means protecting life wherever God has placed us. It could be standing up for the unborn, giving a safe place to foster children, or speaking out when the weak are mistreated. These actions may seem small, unnoticed, or costly, but God honors those who fear Him more than man.

3. *Shrewdness in Exposing Wrong and Calling to Repentance*

Some women in the Bible used shrewdness not only to preserve life but also to expose hidden sin and move others toward repentance. These stories are complex and, at times, unsettling, yet they reveal how God works through shrewd discernment, especially when all other means have failed.

Consider Tamar in Genesis 38. Twice widowed and denied the justice due to her under the law of levirate marriage, Tamar had been wronged by her father-in-law, Judah. He promised her in marriage to his youngest son, but years passed, and he never fulfilled his word. In that culture, childlessness meant poverty and disgrace. Judah ignored her plight, content to let her fade away back in her father's house. Her own father did not intervene either. Without sons, something Judah's sons and later Judah himself denied her, Tamar was without an inheritance or family tree.

So Tamar devised a plan. When she heard that Judah's wife had died, she disguised herself and sat beside the road where she knew he would pass. Mistaking her for a prostitute, Judah slept with her. She kept his staff and seal as a pledge of payment and then disappeared. Later, when her pregnancy became known, Judah—blind to his own guilt—ordered her to be burned. Only then did Tamar send him his own staff and seal with the message, "'By the man to whom these belong, I am pregnant'" (Genesis 38:25).

In that moment, Judah's hypocrisy was exposed. He confessed, "She is more righteous than I . . ." (Genesis 38:26). Tamar's method was troubling, and her deception cannot be excused as righteous in itself, yet her shrewdness forced Judah to confront his sin. God used her courage to bring him to repentance and to preserve the family line that would lead to King David and, ultimately, to Jesus Christ. It is a gross and unsettling story, to say the least, and yet even here we see God's mercy and kindness toward her.

Rebekah's story is just as unconventional. From the moment she conceived twins, God told her that the older son would serve the younger (Genesis 25:23). She carried that word in her heart for decades. Yet when her husband, Isaac, then old and blind, prepared to bless their older son, Esau, she recognized the danger. Esau had already despised his birthright and married pagan wives, thus rejecting the God of Israel. To bless Esau would mean passing God's covenant promises into unfaithful hands.

Isaac seemed determined, so Rebekah intervened. She instructed Jacob to wear Esau's clothes, prepared the meal Isaac expected, and bore the responsibility for the deception on herself, saying, "Let your curse be on me, my son . . ." (Genesis 27:13). Isaac was deceived and blessed Jacob, not Esau. Though the family fractured in the aftermath, God's Word was fulfilled. Jacob became Israel, and the covenant promises continued through him. Rebekah's actions may look manipulative on the surface, but at their core, they were shrewd steps to protect God's covenant promises.

In *Primeval Saints: Studies in the Patriarchs of Genesis*, James B. Jordan calls Rebekah "the great heroine of Genesis."[8] Her name, *Ribqah*, echoes the Hebrew root for "bless." True to her name, Rebekah acted faithfully to preserve God's covenant with His people, even when Isaac erred in his judgment. Like the midwives, Rebekah could not control what happened before or after, but she was faithful to the part of the story that it was within her power to influence.

These stories remind us that shrewdness is sometimes required not only for protection, but for confrontation. Tamar risked her life to expose Judah's inaction and hypocrisy. Rebekah risked her reputation and household peace to prevent Isaac from undermining God's covenant promises. Neither woman had official power or public authority. Both worked indirectly, relying on timing, courage, and shrewdness rather than force.

For Christian women today, this kind of shrewdness means being alert to the sins others ignore and acting with discernment to bring them into the light. In a home, it may mean confronting hidden sin at the right time with carefully chosen words. In a workplace, it may mean refusing to cover dishonesty even when it costs advancement. In the church, it may mean lovingly standing up for key points of biblical doctrine and not turning a blind eye if leaders or ministry partners preach a gospel contrary to that of Jesus Christ, including on key issues of sexuality, marriage, or social justice narratives. Shrewdness does not excuse sin or justify manipulation, but it does teach us when to wait, when to speak, and how to act in ways that protect truth and press others toward repentance.

In each case, whether in judgment and preparation, protecting life, or exposing wrong, biblical women acted shrewdly because they feared God more than man. And God honored their faithfulness, blessing them in their lifetimes or in the unfolding story of redemption. Their examples show us that shrewdness is not manipulation or self-preservation, but courageous wisdom directed toward the good of God's people and His promises to us.

Of course, as my friend Courtney pointed out, "Following biblical principles doesn't guarantee safety or success. Sacrifice and suffering may be required. Women need to be prepared for bold choices, even unto death." This is why I chose to dive deeply into the stories of so many women in the Bible, including many lesser-known characters. I have always loved the Old Testament because the stories are not didactic "do this, not that" teachings, like some parts of girl-boss feminism or the tradwife movement, but are complicated stories that invite us to face God's Word head on. We see the brokenness of humanity as people wrestle with sin, pride, lust, fear, and ambition. Most of all, we see God's character and who He is radiate from its pages.

From Midwives to Modern Witnesses

These biblical stories remind us that shrewdness takes shape in real moments of risk and courage. The same threefold framework that describes the wisdom of biblical women also sheds light on faithful resistance in our own time. From undercover journalism to hidden rooms, from coded songs to sting operations, these modern examples mirror the discernment, protection, and confrontation we see in the Bible.

Shrewdness often begins with discernment, which is the ability to see through deception, to weigh motives, and to prepare carefully before acting. In recent years, conservative commentator Matt Walsh demonstrated this kind of shrewdness in his 2024 documentary *Am I Racist?* Rather than confronting leaders in the anti-racism movement with blunt accusations, Walsh went undercover, giving them space to reveal their own inconsistencies. His questions were pointed but calm, allowing his interviewees to expose the financial and ideological exploitation underlying much of the movement. Walsh did not need to shout to make his point. Instead, like Lady Wisdom in Proverbs, he relied on careful preparation, judgment of character, and a strategy that left the truth standing in plain sight.

This is the same kind of discernment ordinary believers need. Whether it's parents who review their children's textbooks, employees who notice contradictions in corporate trainings, or church leaders weighing which voices to platform, all must practice shrewd preparation. Like Walsh, they do not need to manufacture conflict. They need to recognize folly, give it room to show itself, and be ready to reveal the truth with clarity.

In the pro-life movement, shrewdness has often taken the form of undercover work. Lila Rose, the founder and president of Live Action, entered Planned Parenthood clinics with hidden cameras as a young adult. Sometimes she posed as a teenager impregnated by an older man, or sometimes a member of her organization went undercover as a woman seeking a late-term abortion. Again and again, the footage captured employees offering to ignore mandatory reporting laws, advising on how to cover abuse, or casually discussing procedures the organization denied performing. In one case, an employee explained how to obtain an abortion beyond the legal gestational limit, contradicting the clinic's public stance. These acts were risky, but Rose's aim was clear: protect vulnerable girls and reveal abortion for what it is.

David Daleiden followed similar methods. He posed as a biomedical executive and held meetings with abortion providers. In the recordings, executives discussed how to alter abortion procedures to preserve fetal tissue, even negotiating prices for aborted baby parts. One video showed an executive sipping wine while describing how to crush a fetus in ways that saved the valuable organs. The shock was in the casual tone that normalized a horrific procedure. Daleiden's methods drew lawsuits and his own arrest, yet a court later cleared him, recognizing his tactics as protected investigative journalism. His work pushed the issue of fetal body part sales into national headlines and fueled efforts to strip Planned Parenthood of federal funding.

This kind of shrewd resistance has historical precedent. Harriet Tubman used disguises, false routes, and coded songs to lead enslaved men and women to freedom on the Underground Railroad before the Civil War. She told stories of carrying live chickens so she could pretend to chase them when approached, deflecting suspicion from the fugitives with her.

Corrie ten Boom and her family built a false wall in their home to hide Jews from Nazi soldiers during World War II. They forged documents, lied during interrogations, and risked death if discovered. Corrie later admitted these actions were never easy, but each act of deception was driven by love of neighbor and faithfulness to God's higher law.

Shrewdness in these cases did not mean recklessness. It meant careful preparation, deliberate risk, and creative strategies to save lives. Like the midwives in Egypt or Rahab in Jericho, these more modern examples show that fearing God more than man often requires cunning to frustrate evil and protect the vulnerable.

Other times, shrewdness is needed not only to save life but to uncover wrongdoing. Tim Ballard, whose work inspired the 2023 film *Sound of Freedom*, infiltrated trafficking networks to rescue children. He posed as a buyer, staged elaborate stings, and arranged deals so traffickers would expose themselves. These methods were dangerous and controversial. Yet Ballard's conviction was simple: "God's children are not for sale."[9] The deception created opportunities for law enforcement to intervene and children to be freed.

The unease surrounding Ballard's tactics mirrors the tension in biblical stories like Tamar's and Rebekah's. Both used disguise or deception to expose sin and preserve God's covenant promises. Tamar confronted Judah with his hypocrisy; Rebekah forced Isaac to reckon with God's word about Jacob. Their methods were unsettling, but their aim was faithful. In the same way, Ballard's undercover work illustrates how shrewdness can confront hidden evil that polite or straightforward methods could never reach.

This principle extends beyond global operations. Shrewd confrontation is needed in homes, workplaces, and churches. A woman who suspects financial corruption may need to document carefully before confronting the person. A member of a church who suspects a doctrinal drift may need to gather evidence and approach the right leaders rather than act impulsively or just complain and gossip about the problem rather than confronting those who are in sin (Matthew 18:15–20) or volunteering to serve. A mother who sees sin patterns forming in her husband or children must weigh when to wait, when to speak, and how to do so in a way that leads to repentance rather than rebellion. Like Tamar, Rebekah, and Ballard, shrewdness here means using discernment to bring hidden wrong into the light so that God's truth can be revealed.

Shrill or Shrewd—It's Your Choice

In the same way we explored the legacy of Lady Folly in the Old Testament, her efforts are still alive and well today and directly contradict biblical shrewdness, a virtue tied closely to discernment and godly wisdom. If biblical shrewdness builds through foresight, memory, and disciplined strength, girl-boss feminism often offers its opposite: rage.

This message is not hidden. Soraya Chemaly's book *Rage Becomes Her* frames anger as "an assertion of rights and worth," an essential energy women must reclaim.[10] Brittney Cooper, author of *Eloquent Rage: A Black Feminist Discovers Her Superpower*, notes in her "The Problem with Sass" book chapter the moment she realized "anger could be a powerful force for good," insisting that indignation gave her courage to speak out and resist.[11] *Ms. Magazine* celebrated "The Transformative Power of Women's Anger," telling readers that rage is both authentic and necessary.[12] Academic journals such as *Women's Studies International Forum* go further, presenting female anger as a revolutionary force with political legitimacy.[13] The thread running through all this literature is consistent: feminine anger is a woman's most effective tool, which is why the so-called patriarchy doesn't want you to know about it.

Neuroscience sharpens the biblical warning. A 2024 study from the University of Oregon found that participants induced into angry states recalled fewer details of a story than calm participants, with anger impairing accuracy more than even fear.[14] Research published in the *Journal of Personality and Social Psychology* confirmed that anger narrows attentional scope, driving people to focus only on emotionally charged details while neglecting broader context.[15] Longitudinal studies go further: one in *Frontiers in Psychiatry* (2021) showed that persistent anger symptoms in older adults were associated with sharper declines in episodic memory and executive function, especially in women.[16] Wisdom requires the ability to remember clearly, weigh evidence, and learn from experience. Rage erodes all three.

The effects extend beyond cognition. Chronic anger keeps the body's stress-response system activated—raising blood pressure, flooding the bloodstream with cortisol, disrupting sleep cycles, and suppressing immune defenses. A meta-analysis in the *Journal of the American College of Cardiology* linked hostility and anger to significantly higher risks of coronary heart disease.[17] Mental health outcomes are no better: sustained anger correlates with increased depression, anxiety, and burnout.[18] What begins as a short-term surge of energy becomes, over time, a posture of depletion. The feminist claim that rage "builds" empowerment overlooks the science that shows it actually consumes body, mind, and spirit.

Notably, none of the wise women of Scripture employed rage to accomplish their purposes. Imagine if Miriam had screamed at Pharaoh's daughter, or Rahab had cursed the king's men, or the midwives had relied on the so-called "transformative" power of their rage to undo Pharaoh's unjust laws. They would have been silenced on the spot, if not executed. Picture Rebekah browbeating Isaac into blessing Jacob such that her anger would only have hardened Isaac's resistance; or in the case of Tamar, given Judah just cause to alienate her. In every case, such feminine rage would have been either useless or deadly—the equivalent of that *Parks and Recreation* scene with the Cuban dictator responding to every infraction with "straight to jail," and likely off with their head, too.

Girl-boss feminism's fixation on rage mirrors Jezebel—who was eventually thrown down, trampled, and eaten by dogs after her murderous and manipulative rule—more than these faithful women. Feminine rage promises empowerment, but both science and the Bible reveal its costs: impaired memory, clouded judgment, weakened health, broken relationships, and, ultimately, destruction. Anger may feel clarifying in the moment, but as a strategy, it corrodes the very things women most need to flourish. "The wisest of women builds her house, but folly with her own hands tears it down" (Proverbs 14:1).

Conclusion

What our world and the Church need now more than ever are godly women who walk in the fear of the Lord, practice unrelenting obedience to His Word, and know with clarity who the real enemy is: Satan and the forces of evil that seek to "steal and kill and destroy" the abundant life offered in Christ Jesus (John 10:10). When applied in submission to God and His Word, this posture enables women to grow in discernment, learning to embrace what is true, right, and lovely, and to reject what is false, wrong, and sinful.

Such discernment equips women to engage shrewdly with the world around them, never confusing biblical shrewdness with manipulation, self-serving deception, or rage masquerading as empowerment. From here, wise women move naturally into the third principle of resourcefulness, from which we learn how to place first things first and honor the first domain God entrusted to women: the home.

The greatest examples of shrewd women are not those who subvert God's law or advance their own causes, but those who, in humble submission to His Word, practice shrewd judgment and preparation, protect life at all costs, and find godly ways to expose wrong and create space for repentance. These are the women who, like Amy Carmichael, the Egyptian midwives, or Rahab, embody what it means to be "wise as serpents and innocent as doves"—fearless in obedience, fruitful in faith, and faithful to the God who blesses shrewdness offered for His glory.

PRINCIPLE THREE

Resourcefulness

But Jael the wife of Heber took a tent peg, and took a hammer in her hand. Then she went softly to him and drove the peg into his temple until it went down into the ground while he was lying fast asleep from weariness. So he died. And behold, as Barak was pursuing Sisera, Jael went out to meet him and said to him, "Come, and I will show you the man whom you are seeking." So he went in to her tent, and there lay Sisera dead, with the tent peg in his temple.

—Judges 4:21–22

In the autumn of 1973, the Illinois State Capitol in Springfield became an unlikely battlefield. As legislators prepared to vote on the ratification of the Equal Rights Amendment (ERA)—an amendment that had already passed both houses of Congress and was steamrolling toward ratification—one woman led the opposition's charge. Poised, articulate, and clad in a tailored dress with pearls on her neck, Phyllis Schlafly looked nothing like the political revolutionaries of her time.

The 1970s was a time of profound cultural and political upheaval in America. The sexual revolution, second-wave feminism, and Cold War anxieties collided in the public square. Betty Friedan's book *The Feminine Mystique* had ignited widespread discontent among American housewives, catalyzing the women's liberation movement and setting the stage for political reform. Among the movement's most ambitious goals was the ERA, a proposal to enshrine gender equality into the Constitution with only twenty-four simple words: "Equality of rights under the law shall not be denied or abridged by the United States or by any State on account of sex."[1]

To many Americans, the ERA seemed like common sense as a simple extension of the civil rights movement to women. By 1973, thirty states had ratified the amendment, and momentum seemed unstoppable. Political elites, media institutions, and major women's organizations rallied behind it. Schlafly, then forty-nine years old, appeared to be no match for such a juggernaut. She had no staff, no grants, and no institutional support behind her. What she had, however, was conviction, strategic wit, and a powerful vision of family flourishing.

In her view, the ERA's bland and neutral wording concealed its radical consequences: drafting women into combat, loss of spousal benefits and protections for mothers, and the erosion of legal distinctions that safeguarded women's roles in family, athletics, and society. In her estimation, the ERA wasn't about equality; it was about sameness—and sameness, she argued, was the enemy of both justice and nature.

Schlafly had no office in the formal sense. She worked from her home, with multiple telephones ringing off the hook and children frequently nearby, as her daughter Anne described to me in one conversation. Yet her grasp of political craft was formidable. She organized her volunteers with military precision—referring to them as "combat units"—training them in public speaking, debate, and professional presentation. She held conferences to equip ordinary women for extraordinary public action.

By 1982, the deadline for ERA ratification expired. It fell just three states short. What had seemed inevitable in 1973 had been soundly defeated, due in large part to one woman's leadership in and for the home.

What I love about Schlafly's legacy is that she taught women how to use the tools and resources in their hands to faithfully defend their family, their faith, and the American way of life. Unlike the feminist movement, Schlafly and her followers did not turn to academia to argue for so-called liberation apart from one's sex or family; nor did she teach women that marriage, children, and homemaking were a barrier to their advocacy.

Many hardcore feminists placed *second* things first. They prioritized pressure campaigns in the name of equality, career advancement to break the glass ceiling, and efforts to redefine the family around free love, hook-up culture, and homosexuality. Schlafly, by contrast, taught women to turn the gifts of family, homemaking, and community involvement into a powerful movement. That movement ultimately succeeded.

Thus, our third principle for wise women is resourcefulness: faithfully using the tools, skills, and responsibilities God has *already* placed in your hands within the ordinary spheres of home and community. It grows out of a life rooted in obedience to God, attentiveness to your season, and a readiness to act decisively—even in broken or imperfect circumstances.

One of the clearest examples of resourcefulness comes from the biblical story of Jael. Like Schlafly, she did not seek to be a public figure or a warrior. She lived and worked within her home. Yet when the moment came, she used the very tools of her daily life to bring down the enemy of God's people. Her story, alongside the Woman of Thebez and Mary, the mother of God, stands out as a pattern for the kind of women we need today: women who know what time it is, who are unafraid to crush sin wherever it rears its ugly head, and who do so not in the spirit of feminism, but in submission to God's Word and faithfulness to their season.

The "Most Blessed of Women"

Jael

There are women in Scripture whose names are known, and then there are women whose names echo—faint at first, until you discover that the ground is shaking where they stood. Jael is one of those women. Her story, brief in verses but powerful in its lessons for women today, comes to us in the middle of one of the most violent and spiritually confused chapters in Israel's history. And yet, what she did reverberates through the pages of redemptive history as she became one of the women to fulfill the prophecy spoken to Adam and Eve in the garden: that the seed of the woman would crush the seed of the serpent. Jael's story is one of faithfulness to her daily duties, resourcefulness, foresight, and crushing the head of God's enemy—quite literally.

We are not told much about her background. Her name, Jael, means "mountain goat," a symbol of strength and agility in difficult terrain. Her name also carries the connotation of "one who ascends," a reflection of her own maturity through this story from "maiden" to "mother." Mountain goats, which may sound like the equivalent of naming your daughter Bertha, were not docile animals. They scaled cliffs, leapt across narrow ravines, and navigated perilous paths with an instinctive balance.

The Bible tells us that Jael was the wife of Heber the Kenite, a man who, in a move of political self-preservation, made peace with Israel's enemy, the Canaanites. Their tents were pitched in proximity to the battlefield, and perhaps Heber expected Israel to lose and wanted to preserve his family. Whatever his motivation, we meet Jael as a tradewife working within her tent. Like Adam, her husband is noticeably absent from the narrative. The Kenites, moreover, were not outsiders to Israel's story. They were descended from Moses's Midianite in-laws, who had joined Israel during the wilderness years and shared in God's blessings. By breaking from his people and siding with Canaan's king, Heber placed his household in opposition to God's people.

Among tent-dwelling people like Jael, one of the female duties was setting up and taking down the tents, an act that required not just strength but skill. Using a wooden mallet, Jael likely hammered the wooden tent peg into sandy and hard patches of earth hundreds, if not thousands, of times. It may seem like a trivial object to the modern eye, but in Jael's world, a tent peg was a tool of survival. And because of her faithfulness to this otherwise mundane task, Jael knew how to aim, strike, and anchor her tents.

It is in this context that Jael's story unfolds in Judges 4. As the battle between Israel and the Canaanites reached its climax, Sisera—the feared general who had oppressed Israel for many years—fled the battlefield on foot. His army had been routed, just as God had promised. His iron chariots, rendered useless by God's intervention, were abandoned. Exhausted, disoriented, and desperate for refuge, he stumbled into the tent-dwelling community of his ally, Heber the Kenite.

As he neared the camp, Jael stepped out of her tent and called to Sisera. Her voice was calm, welcoming, and confident: "Turn aside, my lord; turn aside to me; do not be afraid" (Judges 4:18a).

Once inside, Jael covered him with a blanket. He asked for water; she deftly gave him milk and a soft place to rest. This was intentional; she created a comfortable, nourishing, and safe environment where Sisera would be lulled to sleep after possibly days of fighting with little nutrition.

And if her story wasn't already interesting enough, when Sisera fell asleep, Jael acted. She picked up what she knew best: a tent peg, sturdy and sharp. She took the mallet in her hand. This was not a panicked act. It was the same movement she had made countless times before to fortify her home. Only now, that act would deliver a nation. With one clean, devastating strike, she drove the peg through Sisera's skull and into the ground.

There was no scream. No second blow. Just silence.

What is so notable about this story is that when Jael drove the tent peg through Sisera's head, she was not deviating from her normal life. She wasn't looking to exercise rebellion against a patriarchal society or break a tent-canvas ceiling. She was simply faithful in her work, and when thrust into a moment that demanded courage, she rose to defend her covenantal kin in a time of war.

Imagine the immense physical strength and precision it required to drive a wooden tent peg through a man's *skull.* Had she missed, or failed to kill Sisera, it would have meant certain death for her, and perhaps for their entire community.

Later, as Barak, one of Israel's military leaders, approached, Jael again emerged in the fashion of Lady Wisdom and invited Barak to her tent to show him "'the man whom you are seeking'" (Judges 4:22). And, as the book of Judges testifies, "So on that day God subdued Jabin the king of Canaan before the people of Israel" (Judges 4:23).

Jael acted on behalf of God's covenantal promises and people. Though her methods were unorthodox, the Bible does not condemn or criticize her. Far from it. As the Song of Deborah recounts,

> "Most blessed of women be Jael, the wife of Heber the Kenite, of tent-dwelling women most blessed. He asked for water and she gave him milk; she brought him curds in a noble's bowl. She sent her hand to the tent peg and her right hand to the workmen's mallet; she struck Sisera; she crushed his head; she shattered and pierced his temple. Between her feet he sank, he fell, he lay still; between her feet he sank, he fell; where he sank, there he fell—dead." (Judges 5:24–27).

The title of praise, "most blessed of (or among) women," is reserved for two women in the canonical Bible: Jael and Mary, the mother of God. And in each case, wise matriarchs sing this blessing over them.

Jael did not need to become a warrior to do this. She didn't take up a sword or go undercover to fight in Israel's army. Jael used distinctly feminine means to defeat God's enemy.

While Jael's story is not prescriptive in the literal sense, there are five powerful lessons we should glean from her story.

First, when Jael drove the tent peg through Sisera's head, she was not deviating from her daily chores. In the context of nomadic ancient near-eastern tribes, setting up and taking down tent pegs was a woman's job. It was only *because* she was faithful in this task that she was able to drive the tent peg into Sisera's skull, swiftly defeating Israel's enemy. It is through faithfulness to the duties of her season, not escaping them, that Jael was uniquely equipped to defeat the Canaanite general.

Second, because Jael was aware of the political affairs of Israel, she was able to recognize and engage with Sisera. As he approached her tent, Judges 4:18 tells us that "Jael came out to meet Sisera and said to him, 'Turn aside, my lord; turn aside to me; do not be afraid.'" She didn't have her head buried in the sand, and she certainly didn't act as a passive bystander amid the ongoing war. Although her husband had aligned himself with the Canaanites, turning his back on his ancient ally Israel, Jael had a higher allegiance to God and His people, Israel.

Third, Jael was not an activist, a revolutionary, or a social justice warrior. When she saw Sisera stumble toward her, she didn't protest "Hey hey, ho ho, Jabin's rule has got to go!" She didn't rage against his oppressive regime. She was far more subtle. Jael didn't go looking for a fight, but she was ready to defend her home when, in the time of war, the fight came to her.

Fourth, in some metaphorical sense, Jael is the active yet secondary actor in this story. The tent peg was not merely a household tool; it was the *cornerstone* of the tent itself. This connection to Jesus Christ is unmistakable. Jael's fatal strike reflects the promise of Genesis 3:15, foreshadowing Christ-the-tent-peg-Cornerstone, who defeated Israel's enemy in Jael's time and would eventually crush Satan's head once and for all. The New Testament describes Jesus as "the stone that was rejected by you, the builders, which has become the cornerstone" (Acts 4:11), and Zechariah prophesies, "From him shall come the cornerstone, from him the tent peg, from him the battle bow, from him every ruler—all of them together" (Zechariah 10:4). In Jael's story, her ordinary tent peg foreshadows Christ, the ultimate Tent Peg who anchors His people and crushes the enemy. Today, it reminds us that God equips us with what we need, even in ordinary tools, to stand firm and join His victory over sin and death.

Fifth, Jael was placed in a position she never should have been in. Her husband rejected their covenantal relationship with Israel and was nowhere to be found when Sisera arrived. Barak, Israel's general, delayed obedience to God's call. Sisera arrived in Jael's tent because of the failures of the men who should have protected her. And yet, Jael did not collapse in fear or retreat into passivity. Nor did she act with reckless rage. She discerned her role in the moment and acted decisively, even at great risk to herself. As Abigail Dodds observes in an essay for *Desiring God*,

> We should imitate [Jael] in such a way as to apply the godly principles they followed, but not try to replicate the exact scenarios. In other words, I think it unlikely that many of us will find ourselves in a position to kill our people's sworn enemy after he's fled the battlefield. But I do think we ought to consider if we're the sort of woman who could do such a thing if God asked us to. And on a more fundamental level, are we the sort of godly woman who overcomes her fears, keeps her wits about her, and acts with resourcefulness when called upon? How might we grow into that sort of godly woman?[2]

Jael's story is one of resourcefulness and foresight in the defense of her home and God's people, especially given the limits of a broken world.

She did not shy away when sin came knocking at her door. I shared this in the introduction, but it bears repeating: As one person summarized a Charles Spurgeon sermon on sin in a blog post, "We should not be content," he warned, "to see our sins merely fleeing from us; we should pursue them and drive them into the ground—dead—with a nail." He goes on to say, "Jael was ruthless with her enemy. In the same way we should be ruthless with the sin that wants to entrap us and with the things that stand in the way of us knowing God and making Him known. Our weapon might not be a tent peg and hammer but prayer, worship and obedience."[3]

Jael's ruthless elimination of sin should be a testament to us all in how we jealously protect our own hearts and homes from what Galatians 5:19–21 describes as "repetitive, loveless, cheap sex; a stinking accumulation of mental and emotional garbage; frenzied and joyless grabs for happiness; trinket gods; magic-show religion; paranoid loneliness; cutthroat competition; all-consuming-yet-never-satisfied wants; a brutal temper; an impotence to love or be loved; divided homes and divided lives; small-minded and lopsided pursuits; the vicious habit of depersonalizing everyone into a rival; uncontrolled and uncontrollable addictions; [and] ugly parodies of community" (The Message translation). As Paul goes on to warn, "If you use your freedom this way, you will not inherit God's kingdom." The stakes are high, and like in Jael's time, inaction or compromise with sin will mean spiritual death or harm.

As Christians today, we do not fight "against flesh and blood, but against the rulers, against the authorities, against the cosmic powers over this present darkness, against the spiritual forces of evil in the heavenly places" (Ephesians 6:12). Will we, like Jael, have the courage, foresight, and resourcefulness to confront sin when it threatens our homes, protect the next generation from its lies, and wield the ordinary tools God has given us for the sake of His people?

Of course, it is important to keep in mind a necessary counterbalance. Jael's story is not a call to raise our daughters to be warrior princesses on the frontlines of every cultural or theological battle. As author and professor Joe Rigney frames it in a footnote in his book *The Sin of Empathy: Compassion and Its Counterfeits*,

> The issue is not whether a godly woman is able to rebuke feminist error. She clearly is, and God blesses her for it. The issue is when capitulating and cowardly men put forward godly women instead of rebuking and correcting the error themselves, such as when Barak insists that Deborah lead the army, and loses the glory of the victory as a result. Yes, battles are ugly when women fight, as Lewis wrote in Narnia. But Father Christmas still gave Susan her bow and Lucy her dagger. In other words, when your back's again the wall, it's fitting for Christian women to imitate the unnamed woman in Judges 9 and drop the millstone on the wicked king's head. Or be like Jael and drive a tent peg through the bad guy's temple. But neither example supports the notion that women should aspire to combat, whether physical or ideological.[4]

We want to be women who faithfully serve the Lord, cultivate a godly and peaceful spirit—and are well-equipped to drive a tent peg through sin if the moment requires it. The way to be ready in and out of season is not to reenact fight scenes, but to be faithful to your season and practical responsibilities, whatever those are.

The Woman of Thebez

As the final chapters of Judges unfold, we are confronted once again with Israel's unfaithfulness. Like Jael, the Woman of Thebez finds herself in a battle not of her own making. Yet one that, without her intervention, would have meant the death of her family and community.

Her story begins with Abimelech, the son of Gideon. Gideon was a great deliverer whom God used to defeat the Midianites when they oppressed Israel. Yet, the story of Abimelech is perhaps one of the more disturbing illustrations of how far Israel had fallen. Not merely fighting external enemies, Abimelech rebelled and began to oppress his father's own people.

Desiring to rule in his father's place, he murdered his seventy brothers on a single stone—an act of staggering violence.

After razing Shechem, Abimelech marched on Thebez, a nearby city. The text tells us that "there was a strong tower in the city," and all the men, women, and children fled into it, barricading themselves inside. Abimelech, consistent with his pattern of brutality, approached the tower to set it ablaze. And then, out of the silence of the narrative, one woman acted.

Without fanfare or dialogue, "And a certain woman threw an upper millstone on Abimelech's head and crushed his skull" (Judges 9:53). That is all the narrator gives us, and yet it is enough. Not only did she crush Abimelech's skull, but how she did it is also important. A millstone, like the tent peg, was a domestic tool, used for grinding grain. It is heavy, round, and often made of basalt or limestone. The upper millstone would have been small enough to carry but still requiring considerable strength and skill to wield. It was not a weapon of war. It was not forged in a smithy or blessed by a priest. It was a tool of nourishment, homemaking, and faithful labor. And yet, in the Woman of Thebez's hands, it becomes the very thing that brings down a tyrant. The scene unfolded with poetic irony. The man who had killed his brothers on a stone was himself struck down by one.

Mortally wounded but still conscious, Abimelech immediately called to his armor-bearer and said, "Draw your sword and kill me, lest they say of me, 'A woman killed him.'" (Judges 9:54). The Bible does not honor his request. The narrator tells us without embellishment: "Thus

God returned the evil of Abimelech . . ." (Judges 9:56). The final word belongs to God.

The Woman of Thebez didn't wake up looking to kill a loud-mouthed warrior, and her self-defense had none of Abimelech's Jay-Gatsby-esque ambition and scheming. Yet the woman wins. The Woman of Thebez was minding her business, and yet, when dragged into a struggle for her family's life, she humiliated the self-important, self-proclaimed king of Israel. In some sense, this woman was the strong tower of the city. She stood firm, she protected her fellow women and children, and she refused to yield to wickedness.

Mary

If Jael and the Woman of Thebez demonstrate how God delivers His people through the faithfulness of women in times of national crisis, then Mary, the earthly mother of Jesus, shows us the theological fulfillment of God's promise in Genesis 3:15 that the seed of the woman would crush the serpent's head. And yet, her setting is not a battlefield or a besieged city. It is in a small home in a small town. Her tools are the ordinary implements of daily life, including chores, conversation, prayer, and the duties of a young, betrothed woman.

The Gospel of Luke recounts that God sent the angel Gabriel to a town in Galilee called Nazareth, to a virgin named Mary, who was betrothed to Joseph, a descendant of King David. Though the text does not specify what Mary was doing when Gabriel appeared, it implies she was at home. It is easy to imagine her engaged in an ordinary task such as grinding grain, fetching water, tending to household duties, or perhaps praying in private. The divine interruption of this domestic moment was deliberate. God spoke to her while she faithfully fulfilled the chores and duties before her.

As told in Luke 1:28–29, Gabriel greeted Mary, saying, "Greetings, O favored one, the Lord is with you!" But Mary was "greatly troubled at the saying, and tried to discern what sort of greeting this might be." To be "favored" by God is not, in the Bible, to be coddled or exalted in human terms. It is to be set apart for suffering, sacrifice, and faithful obedience.

When the angel revealed that she would conceive and bear a son, and that this son will be called "Son of the Most High . . . of his kingdom there will be no end," (Luke 1:32–33) her response was one of wonder. "How will this be," she asked, "since I am a virgin?" (Luke 1:34). She knew a baby couldn't be conceived without a man, but she still believed that what God said could happen. Mary's question reflects her faith seeking understanding. Saint Bernard of Clairvaux once wrote that there were three miracles at the Annunciation: that God became man, that a virgin conceived, and, perhaps the greatest of the three, that Mary believed.

And believe she did. Her final words to the angel were as simple as they are kingdom-shattering: "Behold, I am the servant of the Lord; let it be to me according to your word" (Luke 1:38). In that moment, she became the new Eve. Rather than rebelling against God's Word, she faithfully submitted to God and His unorthodox timing. Unlike Eve, she did not grasp for divinity, and yet by her submission received the divine into herself. In the act of bearing the Christ-child, she became the vessel through whom the serpent's head would finally be crushed once and for all.

Mary then arose and visited her cousin Elizabeth, and here, the pattern of intergenerational blessing continued. Just as Deborah spoke over Jael, so now Elizabeth, filled with the Holy Spirit, confirmed and magnified Mary's calling. "Blessed are you among women, and blessed is the fruit of your womb!" (Luke 1:42). Once again, the Bible calls a woman "blessed" for her role in delivering God's people.

Mary did not need to escape her pending marriage or wait until she was free from the constraints of the home, childbearing, or small-town life. Her obedience within those exact circumstances became the very means of her role in Jesus Christ's redemption of the world. As Martin Luther wrote, "What you do in your house is worth as much as if you did it up in heaven for our Lord God. . . . We should accustom ourselves to think of our position and work as sacred and well-pleasing to God, not on account of the position and work, but on account of the word and faith from which the obedience and the work flow."[5] Such resourcefulness in the home and attentiveness to material needs continued throughout Mary's life. At the wedding in Cana, where Jesus performed His first recorded miracle, it was Mary who prompted His intervention, instructing the servants to do whatever He said so the host would be spared embarrassment.

Though both Jael and Mary are called "blessed among women," their stories are not equal. Just as Joshua was a type of Christ but not His equal, and as Moses and John the Baptist were forerunners who prepared the way but could not complete it, so too Jael's deliverance points forward to a greater one. The New Covenant does not erase the old; it fulfills and glorifies it. What was bronze in Judges becomes gold in the Gospels. In the Old Covenant, Israel's victories were won through violence and were always temporary. Each triumph was followed by another fall. But in Mary, we see the beginning of a new kind of victory: the triumph of faith, obedience, and surrender. The battle is no longer fought with tent pegs or millstones but through the yielding of a faithful heart to God's will. Thus, in many ways, Mary is the true and greater Jael. Where Jael drove a stake through Sisera's head, Mary bore the One who crushed the serpent's head forever. Where Jael's act brought fleeting peace to Israel, Mary's obedience brought eternal peace to the world.

Jael was a married woman, the Woman of Thebez may have been widowed, and Mary was a virgin. And in each case, God called and used them mightily for His purposes. It's a beautiful reminder that whatever season you are in, God can and will use you, too.

Their examples remind us that femininity isn't something to overcome or set aside for God to use you. It is, when rightly ordered, one of the most powerful tools in His kingdom. Jael's resourcefulness secured a military victory. The Woman of Thebez, surrounded by families cowering in a tower, reached for a millstone and ended a tyrant's reign. And Mary, standing in a simple home, said yes and brought forth the Savior of the world.

Hollywood Missed the Memo—Again

When we picture a woman fighting for a cause, it is almost always filtered through modern media: Mulan, the Woman King, Wonder Woman, Captain Marvel, Katniss Everdeen in *The Hunger Games*, Rey in *Star Wars*, or Black Widow. These stories share a common theme: to be powerful, a woman must fight like a man. She must strap on armor, wield a sword, shoot arrows, or stand toe-to-toe with men who are twice her size.

Some of these stories, like Mulan's, resonate on a deep level. As the eldest daughter, I've always felt connected to Mulan's sacrificial instinct to protect her family. That fearless love is certainly feminine. But the movie ultimately suggests her strength must be proven by winning on masculine terms, dressed in masculine armor. It misses the unique ways women fight and lead, including the resourcefulness of Jael, the Woman of Thebez, and the surrendered faith of Mary, each of whom relies on feminine and household tools to defeat the enemy.

In *The Woman King*, a fictional band of female warriors trains and fights like men going sword to spear and strength against strength. Watching such stories can be exhilarating, but it also leaves you asking: where are the men? Yes, there have at different times and places been exceptional women who fought in battle, but those moments are the exception, not the norm. The biological reality is clear: women are generally smaller, with less muscle mass and explosive physical force than men. That does not diminish female dignity; it simply points to the truth that physical combat is not the primary arena in which feminine strength shines brightest.

The message, explicit or implied, is this: if a woman wants to protect her people, she must outdo men at their own game. Meanwhile, more feminine forms of strength—persuasion, foresight, resourcefulness, community-building, hospitality, and the extraordinary feat of bearing children, literally offering one's body and blood to bring forth new life—are ignored or diminished.

Tragically, the evangelical church has often swallowed the same lie. From conference stages to women's ministry books, we hear the recycled slogan that "women can have it all." Consider Senator Katie Britt's widely circulated *Wall Street Journal* interview "The Conservative Women Who Are 'Having It All'" (August 2025). In 2021, when she was deciding whether to run for the Senate as a Republican from Alabama, she admitted she wrestled with the cost: "Just missing those moments and not being present for everything. I really wrestled with it. The world is full of voices saying this can't work." Yet the story pivots at her daughter's words: "Mom, you have to do this. . . . Doesn't God call on you to do hard things?"[6]

That line has been praised in Christian and conservative circles as an anthem of courage, but notice what it leaves unchallenged: the assumption that faithfulness must look like leaving the home to prove oneself in public life. Instead of dignifying the home as a primary place of leadership and influence, this narrative casts motherhood and household stewardship as obstacles to overcome, not assignments to embrace. It's the same tired rhetoric the world pushed a decade ago, now recycled in evangelical dress. And it leaves us with the same haunting questions: Is your own home in order? Are you seeking godly counsel and learning to be a productive, faithful steward of what God has placed in your hands? That is where resourcefulness begins.

Our interruptions or setbacks are often His invitations. Sometimes they call us to adjust our posture, to move forward with open hands and a gracious heart. Other times, they signal that we're trying to do too much in a season that calls for less formal work and more available time with family.

To take this from idea to practice, let's turn to the tent peg strategy for resourceful women.

The Tent Peg Strategy: Living Out Faithfulness Today

We must first recognize the moment we're living in. If the home front is neglected, everything else eventually unravels. With that in mind, there are a few guiding principles to consider as we reflect on what it means to be a resourceful woman today.

1. Resourcefulness Starts at Home

Like Jael, we must confront the battles inside the tent before looking outward. That may mean facing a pattern of sin, bitterness, or distraction within our own households. Prayer, Scripture, and accountability are the tools God has given us to begin restoring order and faithfulness where we live.

2. Resourcefulness Also Means Using What Is Already in Your Hand

Instead of wishing for someone else's gifts or opportunities, ask what skills, relationships, or resources God has already entrusted to you. It might be something simple: hospitality, prayer, teaching, organization, or encouragement. Even small, hidden acts of faithfulness can bless others and build God's kingdom.

3. Seasons Matter

Like Mary, we are called to embrace the season we are in rather than despising it or rushing ahead. Whether as a student, worker, mother, or caregiver, each role is God's present assignment. Resourcefulness does not look past today in search of something grander. It asks, How can I be faithful right here? Notably, Schlafly did not step into her public role through the ERA fight until her children were grown.

4. Preparation Matters Too

The Woman of Thebez did not set out planning to defeat a tyrant, but when the moment came, she was ready. Resourceful women keep themselves sharp through spiritual disciplines, learning, and watchfulness. This is not about chasing ambition but about being prepared to act wisely when God opens a door.

5. Faithful Resourcefulness Avoids Extremes

The world says to fight like a man. Some in the church say to stay quiet and uninvolved. Both are distortions. True resourcefulness walks between passivity and ambition, trusting God's design while refusing to waste the opportunities He gives.

6. Leadership Through Service Is Another Mark

Phyllis Schlafly's "war room" was her living room. Influence often occurs in small places: opening a home, mentoring another woman, serving in church, or praying over neighbors. The world celebrates power on platforms; God often works through tables and living rooms.

7. Resourceful Women Trust God with the Outcome

Jael, the Woman of Thebez, and Mary all acted faithfully with what they had. None could control the results. They simply did what was before them, and God brought victory and blessing.

Conclusion

The key to understanding Schlafly, and all wise women, is to understand their lives through the lens of *seasons*. The arc of a woman's life is long. We mature quickly, and on average, we live longer than men. So instead of adopting the life script pushed by modern universities and girl-boss feminism—one that pressures women to pursue the highest levels of education and professional achievement all at once, and as early as possible—a seasonal view offers something wiser and more humane.

Schlafly lived this kind of life. It allowed her to prioritize first things first: raising children during the crucial early years, working and volunteering as time allowed, and gradually shifting her public commitments as her children grew older. This model of traditional womanhood encourages public engagement, but only after family duties have been honored.

And this is precisely why Phyllis Schlafly's story matters for us today. She didn't win by acting like a man. She didn't abandon her home, her femininity, or her faith. She led through them. Her army was made up of volunteers, often mothers, trained in persuasion, hospitality, and disciplined engagement. She understood how to use the tools God had given her, and she taught others to do the same.

This is the kind of womanhood we need to recover: a generation of wise women rising in faithful obedience using the tools God has placed before them to crush the heads of sin, shame, and evil that are around us.

This work begins at home—with a husband or with roommates, with children or with fellow Christians—and its influence ripples outward. It reaches elders and kings. It shapes churches, and even, in time, the direction of nations. The women God uses don't naturally pick up the sword to fight, nor do they seek to replace the men God has called to lead. Yet they are indispensable in God's redemptive work.

It is no coincidence that, as I sat down to write this chapter, my oldest daughter came down with a cold and fever, and my youngest hit the infamous four-month sleep regression. Within a day, I went from two children sleeping on schedule to long, sleepless nights and unpredictable mornings. I typically begin my work very early, rising before the girls wake so I can be present with them during the day. But that particular morning, as I tried to pray the morning psalms about offering a sacrifice of thanksgiving, I found myself repenting—again and again—for frustration and resentment. My youngest kept waking before dawn, just as I would sit back down to write. I had things to do—important things, I told myself.

And yet, the Lord reminded me: that *is* the important work.

It's easy to write about how God uses home, family, and children to reveal His calling on our lives. It's another thing entirely to believe that when your children seem to be pulling you away from the "real work." But when I start resenting my children, it's a clear sign that my heart and my priorities have drifted. Yes, deadlines are real. And yes, responsibilities matter. But ultimately, I must trust that as I love and care for my girls in this season, God will give me grace for the rest. He'll provide the strength to complete the work—or the humility to ask for an extension.

I share this because the battle so often begins right here in the ordinary moments of late-night homework, loads of laundry, secluded breastfeeding sessions, and family prayer. The same God who worked through Jael in her tent, the Woman of Thebez in her tower, and Mary in her home is at work in our lives, too. Their stories remind us that faithfulness in small things is the foundation for God's victories over sin, shame, and death.

Because when women walk in obedience to God—yes, even in the small, unseen corners of their homes—the kingdom of God advances. Serpents are crushed. Legacies are built. And princes are cast down.

PRINCIPLE FOUR

Hospitality

And when the king saw Queen Esther standing in the court, she won favor in his sight, and he held out to Esther the golden scepter that was in his hand. Then Esther approached and touched the tip of the scepter. And the king said to her, "What is it, Queen Esther? What is your request? It shall be given you, even to the half of my kingdom." And Esther said, "If it please the king, let the king and Haman come today to a feast that I have prepared for the king."

—Esther 5:2–4

Growing up, I was captivated by the charm and romance of colonial and Victorian cultures, from Jane Austen's idyllic English countryside and elegant balls to the resilient pioneer women forging new lives in the early American republic. Even as a child, I was drawn to the parts of these worlds where people gathered, whether around long tables for meals, in parlors for conversation, or on a front porch to share tea. At summer camps, I eagerly learned sewing, embroidery, knitting, tea etiquette, and dancing. I did not realize then that these skills would one day become tools for welcoming others. My adventures also included camping trips where we built fires, cooked outdoors, and constructed forts, always making sure everyone had a place to join in.

My husband and his brothers remember their childhoods differently. They reenacted the Continental Army's encampment at Valley Forge in snow-covered tents, planned strategic maneuvers, and governed their imagined "Boys' Republic" of fifteen neighborhood kids. Yet even in their play, community was at the center. They shared meals, formed alliances, and told stories around imagined campfires. Looking back, I see that our happiest memories, his and mine alike, have always revolved around bringing people together. Those early moments planted the seed of the joy I now find in hosting and hospitality.

For many children, pretend play is often about hosting. We set up tea parties, build forts, and invite others in. But as we grow older and our schedules fill, we forget the power of making space to truly welcome others. Playing outside until dinner turns into travel ball and meals eaten in the car. Family dinners shrink into single plates balanced in front of screens. Our homes begin to feel like private retreats instead of places entrusted to us to gather and care for the needs of others.

Ironically, we spend more time watching cooking shows and scrolling social media than ever before, and yet, instead of it drawing us into community, it further isolates us as rates of obesity, depression, and loneliness climb. There are many factors contributing to this, but what is for sure is that a renewed practice of life-giving hospitality is, at least in part, the remedy.

That is why the fourth principle is hospitality. It means opening our homes, setting our tables, and creating space to care for the physical, spiritual, and emotional needs of those around us, where simple acts of obedience become God's means of reconciliation, unmasking evil, and bringing new life.

This kind of hospitality moves in two directions, and both matter today. First, it creates sacred spaces of comfort and care where weary people can be seen, heard, and loved. Second, it becomes a form of holy resistance and strategic engagement where women persuade, teach, convict, and win favor with others.

We're tempted to tell ourselves that hospitality can wait until the house is clean, until the schedule lightens, or until we have more money or energy or bandwidth. But biblically, hospitality is not an afterthought. It is a form of spiritual resistance: a way to push back the loneliness, isolation, and exhaustion of modern life. It is also a unique way that women lead and shape history.

This chapter is an invitation to reclaim hospitality as a life-giving and life-shaping force, one that speaks to the heart of what it means to be a wise woman made in God's image. So, come to the table. There's more at stake than you've been led to believe.

One Woman's Hospitality Transforms a Nation

The Book of Esther offers one of the best stories of biblical hospitality. Many know the famous line: "And who knows whether you have not come to the kingdom for such a time as this?" (Esther 4:14). It's quoted on wall art and Instagram, but behind it is a deeper story of courageous leadership and holy resistance through hospitality. Esther didn't save her people by force; she saved them by setting a table.[1]

The Bible describes King Ahasuerus as an insecure and foolish man. The Book of Esther, written with elements of both comedy and tragedy, often uses exaggeration to highlight character flaws and plot turns, such as a six-month-long banquet, the creation of gallows fifty cubits high, or the offer to give Esther half the kingdom, if it would please her. These over-the-top moments point to the instability of a king who tries to mask his insecurity with displays of power.

But I am getting ahead of myself. Esther's story begins with another woman—Queen Vashti. During a drunken feast, King Ahasuerus commanded Vashti to appear before him and his guests. Much like the story of Herod and his niece in the New Testament during John the Baptist's time, the implication seems to be that it is a sensual, degrading, and possibly dangerous request. Vashti refused to come, and the king, embarrassed and enraged, lashed out.

Hoping to deter further outbursts, the council of advisors redirected the King's embarrassment by making this a universal issue, "For the queen's behavior will be made known to all women, causing them to look at their husbands with contempt. . ." (Esther 1:17a). So, King Ahasuerus banished Vashti and sent a decree commanding wives to obey their husbands.

Some time passed, and the king began to miss Vashti, or at least the idea of a queen. His advisors proposed a search for the most beautiful women in the kingdom, setting the stage for Esther and Mordecai.

Esther caught the attention of the king's attendants, for she "had a beautiful figure and was lovely to look at" (Esther 2:7). Accompanied by her cousin Mordecai, who raised her after the death of her parents, the king's attendants brought Esther into the palace to begin her year of preparation.

True to the "maiden" metaphor, Esther earned favor by faithfully obeying Mordecai's guidance. She also did what Hegai, the head eunuch, said and followed his advice with care. When her time came to appear before the king, she found favor not only with him, but with everyone who saw her. In the end, she was chosen to be queen.

To be clear, Esther's success did not come because she was a doormat or just a pretty face. Yoram Hazony aptly points out in his book *God and Politics in Esther* that it was far more strategic than that. Esther's humility and attention to detail showed those around her that she not only valued their insight, but that she could fit in with the king's palace. She learned their customs and navigated the political theater with wisdom. Like Jael, Esther belonged to a long line of women who used discernment, shrewdness, resourcefulness, and hospitality to protect God's people and crush the serpent's head. Her name reflects this: Esther means "star" in Persian, but in Hebrew it means *hester*—to hide—revealing her hidden strength, savvy, and God's providence. While she worked within the palace, Mordecai occupied the king's broader court.

From this strategic position, Mordecai continued to advise Esther and, in a providential moment, overheard a plot to assassinate the king. His warning, passed along to Esther, ultimately saved the king's life. Yet the king forgot to thank Mordecai. Instead, the next chapter begins with the king elevating Haman above all his other advisors, filtering his circle of counselors through one man. When everyone in the court bowed down to Haman, Mordecai refused. He recognized Haman as an existential threat to the kingdom. Moreover, Haman the Agagite was likely a descendant of the Amalekite king Agag, the ancient enemy of Israel, going back to the time of King Saul and King David. Seeing Mordecai's refusal, Haman's wrath was ignited against the entire Jewish people.

He told the king: "'There is a certain people. . . . Their laws are different from those of every other people, and they do not keep the king's laws . . .'" (Esther 3:8). With carefully chosen words, Haman convinced the king to issue a decree authorizing the destruction and plunder of the Jews throughout the empire.

Imagine how surreal this moment must have been for Esther. No one knew that she was a Jew, and yet her own husband had just signed an order that would put her people to death. Without much political influence beyond her station, and the memory of what happened to Vashti likely lurking in her mind, Esther resisted Mordecai's initial plea that she go before the king and beg for his favor. But Mordecai challenged her silence: "'Do not think to yourself that in the king's palace you will escape any more than all the other Jews. . . . And who knows whether you have not come to the kingdom for such a time as this?'" (Esther 4:13–14).

Until that point, the Bible described Esther with passive language: "taken," "told," "directed." But here she becomes an active agent in

God's redemptive work. She matures from maiden to mother, no longer merely obedient, but one who discerns, decides, and leads. Esther moves from a servant in the king's palace to a hostess in her own right.

In response, Esther sent word to Mordecai and instructed him to gather all the Jews in Susa for three days of fasting and prayer. She, along with her attendants, would do the same.

Though she had not been summoned by the king for over a month, Esther approached Ahasuerus at the end of the three-day fast, fully aware that entering his presence uninvited could cost her life. By God's mercy, the king received her graciously. He extended his scepter in pardon, and in front of the court asked her, "'What is it, Queen Esther? What is your request? It shall be given you, even to the half of my kingdom" (Esther 5:3). So, she invited King Ahasuerus and Haman to a feast.

It's a dramatic reversal. Esther, who was not invited, extended an invitation to the King.

This is where Esther's prudent leadership becomes most evident. Esther didn't rush in with legal arguments or wrathful protests or dramatic pleas. She didn't expose Haman in open court or confront the king in anger.

Had she done so, she would have publicly humiliated her husband by revealing that she was a Jew and that he had unknowingly signed a death warrant for his own queen. Such a revelation would likely have turned his heart against her, just as it had once turned against Queen Vashti.

So, instead, she set a table. She invited the king and Haman to a feast. Not once, but twice. She created an atmosphere that was familiar, intimate, and disarming. Hospitality became her act of holy resistance to ultimately reveal Haman's evil plot to destroy God's people.

Esther discerned what many failed to see: that the timing was just as important as the message. She carefully prepared a lavish feast and hosted it with grace. When the king again offered her anything she desired at the first banquet, she waited. The timing wasn't right. Unlike Eve, who grasped at what was withheld, Esther responded with discernment and restraint. She invited the king and Haman to a second feast, where her true plan unfolded.

Perhaps the king was amused by what he saw as his queen's shyness or was simply pleased by the novelty of it all. Whatever the reason, both he and Haman accepted the second invitation with ease. And it is there, at the second feast, that Esther executed her plan.

At the second feast, when the king pressed her for her request, Esther finally unveiled it: "A foe and enemy! This wicked Haman!" (Esther 7:6a). Her words were few, but they struck with precision. Esther clearly discerned good from evil and did not hesitate to name it in Haman.

Esther did not come to the king with forceful demands, long speeches, or wrathful protests. Instead, she subtly won him over through lavish and life-giving hospitality and then chose her moment carefully to reveal the depravity of Haman's plan. He never stood a chance.

At that point, the whole story shifted. Haman, once elevated, fell. Like Jael before her, Esther used discernment, shrewdness, resourcefulness, and hospitality to defeat God's enemy. The very gallows Haman built for Mordecai became the means of his own death. King Ahasuerus, now emboldened as the protector of his wife, reverses the decree and pours out favor on Esther, Mordecai, and the Jewish people.

We often think of hospitality as a private virtue: something domestic, sweet, and perhaps optional. But Esther's story reminds us that it is also a political, and therefore public, act of leadership and social resistance. Esther matured from a maiden to a mother as she skillfully planned, hosted, and won over the king's affection through her feasts. By inviting the king to her feast unannounced, Esther risked her life. For most of us, the greatest risk is discomfort or rejection. And who knows, being a good hostess might save your life.

Esther's story reveals five powerful truths about biblical hospitality and why we must practice it in our own lives today.

1. God Commands Hospitality

Hospitality, represented by the metaphor of the *table*, is not a minor theme in the Bible or a hobby for the extroverted. From Genesis to Revelation, it stands at the center of God's story with His people. It is not just something God *does*; it is an expression of who He *is*. God's story is one of making room, preparing tables, and welcoming the lost, lonely, and wayward home. Whether it's the communion table of the Lord or the many tables throughout the Bible where God meets with His people, God uses hospitality to strengthen, mature, and ultimately protect His people.

God set a table of abundance in Eden, filling it with beauty and provision. As Mark Brians II and Drew Knowles write in *Hospitality: The Convivial Mission of God*, though fully self-sufficient, God "makes room for what is *not* God"—us.[2] Yet Adam and Eve rejected His invitation, choosing to dine with the Accuser instead.[3] Still, God continued His hospitality through manna in the wilderness, water from the rock, and a land flowing with milk and honey.

Jesus carried this same pattern forward. His ministry overflowed with meals alongside sinners, disciples, and strangers. He called Himself the Bread of Life and offered living water to all who thirst. Even after His resurrection, He broke bread at Emmaus, cooked breakfast by the sea, and promised, "And if I go and prepare a place for you, I will come again and will take you to myself, that where I am you may be also" (John 14:3). Heaven is the fullness of that divine welcome.

The early church knew this well: "Seek to show hospitality" (Romans 12:13); "Show hospitality to one another without grumbling" (1 Peter 4:9); "Do not neglect to show hospitality to strangers . . ." (Hebrews 13:2). To practice hospitality is to reflect the very heart of God.

Esther embodied this command. She did not wait for ideal conditions or a royal decree to act; she mirrored God's heart for hospitality, working through distinctly feminine means to achieve victory over Haman.

Like David, her actions declared, "You prepare a table before me in the presence of my enemies" (Psalm 23:5a). Throughout Scripture, faithful hospitality is rarely safe or convenient. God's Word shows us hospitality can be costly, dangerous, and require a self-sacrificial willingness to welcome others in, like the widow who gave her last meal to the prophet Elijah (1 Kings 17:7–16), trusting that God would provide. In this way, Esther shows us how the faithful practice of hospitality, even when we are afraid of being rejected, can alter the course of nations.

2. Hospitality Exposes and Heals Sin

This truth became real to me one Saturday night while Jack was in seminary. I had looked forward to spending the evening together, assuming it was set aside as a much-needed break from work, parenting, and Jack's studies. When I realized he planned to return to work after dinner, I felt rejected. It didn't take long before my disappointment turned to resentment. I decided, rather childishly, to skip making dinner and go watch a movie with friends instead once I put our daughter to bed. I thought, *If Jack didn't have time for me, I would go spend time with those who did.* I know, it was downright petty.

While tidying up, I heard a noise outside our basement window. When I opened the door, a woman stood on our patio, retrieving a wagon she had left there earlier. She was homeless and apologized for the intrusion. Assuring her that it was okay, we introduced ourselves and learned her name: Nicole. As she turned to leave, I felt a sudden nudge from the Holy Spirit and asked, "Are you hungry?" She nodded.

I invited her in and began preparing the meal I had intended for Jack. The three of us—Jack, Nicole, and I—sat together around our small table, eating, talking, and praying. Our daughter briefly joined us, too, sleepy-eyed and curious. In that simple meal, something sacred happened. God replaced my bitterness with repentance and reminded me that His hospitality begins in the home. Had I followed through with my plan, I would have missed the whole thing.

We never saw Nicole again, and I still wonder if she was one of those angels we entertain without knowing (Hebrews 13:2). Yet her visit changed my perspective. The meal turned my gaze outward—away from self-pity and toward the daily, undeserved hospitality of God. He had set a table before me, even in the presence of my own spiritual enemies: pride, anger, and entitlement.

It is no wonder the enemy works so hard to keep us from the table. Few things are as spiritually powerful, or as restorative, as sharing a meal. The table invites honesty. It exposes division. It becomes the place where grace meets truth. As Jack often says, the table is the altar of the home. It is where we worship God through thanksgiving, gratitude, and the breaking of daily bread.

So it was with Esther. Her table became the altar where hidden sin was exposed. What no courtroom argument could achieve, her feast accomplished: Haman's pride, deception, and violence came into the light. Esther's willingness to host and to win the king's favor positioned her to reveal the truth at the moment of greatest influence and to bring healing between the king and God's people. In the same way, our own tables can become places where grace exposes falsehood and restores what is broken.

This is the heart of true hospitality. As Christ invites us to His table, so we open ours to others. It is not optional for the Christian. Every meal becomes a reflection of the Lord's Table and an act of resistance as we replace the scarcity mindset of the world with the abundance of God's kingdom.

3. The Medium Is the Message

Imagine a vintage KFC billboard: a shiny red-and-white bucket of fried chicken stamped with the words "Women's Liberation."[4] The ad, which appeared in the 1970s, captured a cultural turning point. As the feminist movement gained momentum and women stepped beyond traditional domestic roles, corporations saw an opportunity. They marketed fast food not just as convenience, but as freedom from the kitchen and the labor of hospitality.

In reality, the story was more complex. As food writer Michael Pollan notes, companies had been preparing for this moment for decades, developing the technology to preserve and mass-produce food. After World War II, the infrastructure was ready, but the culture was not.[5] When social roles shifted, the industry seized its moment with a simple promise: *Don't worry. We'll do the cooking.*

We can all appreciate the convenience of microwaved meals after a long day or a quick DoorDash order during late-night work. Yet it raises a deeper question: what did we lose when we exchanged the time of preparing and sharing meals for quick consumption? Many traded fresh meals for food laced with pesticides and ultra-processed ingredients, and as *fast* overshadowed *food*, we also devalued the time around the table.

As Marshall McLuhan's famous line reminds us, "the medium is the message."[6] The *how* shapes the *what*. The same is true of hospitality. The medium—how we prepare, share, and host—carries its own message about what we believe. A meal eaten behind the glow of screens says one thing; a homemade meal shared with prayer, people, and an intentional time when we cease from our labor to connect with others says something else. Our methods reveal our theology.

Esther understood this intuitively. The form of her appeal was itself her message. By preparing a feast rather than a protest, she embodied Lady Wisdom's pattern of preparing a feast of fine wine and bread, calling out to the simple to eat with her, and calling out wrongdoing. She humanized herself as the representative of the Jewish people and ingratiated herself to the king. Her own desire was for God's generosity, kindness, and prosperity to be upon her people, as it was upon the table she prepared. And the king, disarmed and emboldened to comply, agreed.

We told ourselves we were freeing women from the burden of the kitchen and opening the door to opportunity, and in part, we were. Yet the trade-off was costly. We surrendered the health of our homes and our capacity to care for the whole person: their body, heart, and soul.

Worse yet, our methods told young women to set hospitality aside in favor of corporate success. As one friend shared with me, while she is thankful her parents prioritized her education and academic success throughout high school, the practical result is that her mother took on all the cooking and dinner responsibilities by herself. Now, as a married mother of two children, she finds herself still learning how to plan, prepare, and serve nourishing meals for her family on a day-to-day basis. She told me that, in retrospect, she wishes her mother had not only encouraged her academic development but also invested in passing along domestic skills, such as cooking and baking, that would now bless her household in tangible ways.

In trying to put more time into women's hands, our culture unintentionally devalued the home itself. As Dr. Casey Means, co-author of *Good Energy: The Surprising Connection Between Metabolism and Limitless Health*, wrote in a recent X post,

> Feminist messaging made the role of food preparation out to be some kind of second-class subservient role and the embodiment of wasted potential. Purpose was found outside the home. . . . The messaging convinced many of us that food preparation is a roadblock in the way of reaching our highest purpose (which is squarely at the top of the corporate ladder). . . . I know this because I grew up with this messaging and judged women harshly who labored in the kitchen for their families as sad and a waste of potential.[7]

As Christians, we do not worship nature or idolize dietary purity, but we do believe in an incarnational God who took on flesh, redeemed it, and called us to steward it well. We do not merely *have* bodies; we *are* embodied creatures. Recovering a holistic view of food preparation and hospitality means making time to care for the spiritual, physical, and emotional needs of the image-bearers seated at our tables.

4. Hospitality Is Social Resistance

When we got married, many places were finally relaxing their coronavirus protocols. Washington, DC, on the other hand, chose that month to enforce vaccine passports. We like to joke that our broader group of friends all lost a bit of weight during that time. Not by choice, but because many of us stopped eating out altogether. Some weren't vaccinated; others protested the mandate on principle. Either way, our social lives shifted from loud, impersonal restaurants to the warmth of each other's homes.

One friend became skilled at mixing cocktails and hosted themed drink nights. We cooked meals, organized game nights, and eventually began celebrating birthdays, engagements, movie nights, and baby showers in our living rooms. We shared dishes, supplies, and split costs—stretching small budgets into some of my favorite memories.

One of the best things to come from that season was the strengthening of Thursday Night Dinners, a weekly ritual that, aside from a brief summer break in 2024, continued unbroken for five years in Washington, DC.

Each Thursday, Chris and Max opened their home to anyone and everyone. What began with slow arrivals, "Venmo the hosts!" reminders, and lamb or pot roast dinners, would end with evening prayer and late nights of deep conversation. These meals were costly as Chris, Max, and others devoted their own money, multiple nights of preparation, and hours in the kitchen to prepare an exquisite meal.

We kept attending even after our first daughter was born, often putting her to bed in an upstairs room. We weren't the only family; Thursday nights drew just-graduated Capitol Hill staffers, young professionals, families, and everyone in between. Some weeks, fifty people showed up. One of the best outcomes was the depth of real, adult friendships. Thursday Dinner became the answer to every unfulfilled "we should get coffee sometime."

As Chris, who led from the beginning, recalls, "Thursday Dinner came about by accident—I always joke people came over and just never left." At first it was a handful of friends eating after church, but during the pandemic, it grew into a lifeline for newcomers. "If we're going to live the lives we hope to live, good friends are essential. And forming good friendships means something practical: you need to be around."

His approach was simple but demanding: "It's here, every week, reliable, free, and I'm cooking you dinner." That consistency came at great cost—thousands of dollars, endless shopping and chopping, and "more than one night of crying from exhaustion." But Chris insisted the food itself mattered: "It's different from canned spaghetti. A good meal says, 'You're worth the effort.'"

What kept him going were the stories: "Whenever I thought about quitting, someone would say, 'This changed everything. I was alone, and now I'm not. I met my spouse. I found friends. I started praying again. I'm going back to church." In the end, the same rules that divided many in the city strengthened our Christian community with greater depth, resourcefulness, and belonging.

Similarly, Esther's hospitality was also an act of resistance. In a court ruled by vanity and fear, she did not argue or accuse; she set a table. Each feast drew the king closer, exposed Haman's pride, and turned the empire's power inside out. In her courage, we see that faithful hospitality is still the most powerful way to resist the social pressure around us and build deeper connections.

5. Hospitality Matures Us and Refines Our Influence

Entire books have been written about hospitality that explore the how, why, and what in greater depth. For this chapter, the goal is to reinforce its essential role as a means of discipleship, social resistance, and feminine influence. That is why hospitality, as an extension of all that has come before, is the fourth principle on the path to becoming a wise woman.

James B. Jordan's illustration of maturity through baking a cake illustrates this progression well. Like Esther, we begin by following each step of the recipe to a T. Mastery of the basics is essential before we improvise too much. Practically, this means reading and learning how to host well, from planning menus and decorating a table to budgeting, grocery shopping, and timing a meal.

As we grow, we gain confidence. We begin to experiment, add our own touches, and make adjustments by feel rather than simply replicating someone else's success. We keep good systems in place, such as frozen cookie dough, tea, or popcorn ready to serve, so we can host at a moment's notice. Over time, our favorite hosting recipes become second nature to us.

Then comes the final stage of wisdom. As Jordan says, "Through trial and error, you acquire wisdom about making a bundt cake. Then, when people praise your cake as especially good, you can write down the recipe for them and instruct them in how to make one."[8] So too with hospitality: as we mature, we mentor others. We move from hosting small gatherings to coordinating larger ones, such as community dinners, seminary events, political fundraisers, or retirement celebrations. Experience gives us poise, allowing us to lead others in serving well beyond our own kitchen.

Esther's story is the pattern of this maturity. She begins as one who follows directions and ends as one who gives them. Her growth, from "maiden" to "mother," from guest to hostess, shows that hospitality is not just a duty but a school of wisdom. She learns when to wait, when to invite, and when to speak. Her table becomes the means by which she leads, persuades, and blesses others.

History offers many examples of this same wisdom at work. Dolley Madison, the wife of the fourth president of the United States, was known as the "Hostess of Washington." Through her elegant dinners and receptions, she united rival factions, advanced public causes, and softened political tensions. She understood what Esther knew: that a well-set table can build alliances, reconcile enemies, and steady nations.

So it is with us. As we mature in hospitality, our tables become places of influence. Rather than relying on formal titles, speeches, or someone else inviting you to share your insight, consistent and life-giving hospitality opens the door to lovingly influence our families, communities, and nation—literally.

The Tent Peg Strategy: Hospitality in Action

True hospitality invites and reveals. It does not require one to be married, have children, or have a picture-perfect home. Far from it. What it does require, however, can be much harder to give: vulnerability, a willingness to see and be seen, and the courage to share yourself with others.

As our former Rector David Glade often said, "You can learn more about someone after thirty minutes in their home than three hours in a coffee shop." Welcoming someone into your home unveils something deeply personal. In many ways, our homes are reflections of our inner life. They reflect what we love, how we live, and what we hold dear.

Mark Brians II and Drew A. Knowles describe this well:

> We are creatures who eat, but eating together requires vulnerability. We risk having our invitation declined. We risk overcooking the meal. We risk the awkwardness of conversation with someone we don't yet know. But make no mistake—we all desperately want to feast together. It's just easier to keep our distance.[9]

More often, we avoid hospitality because it feels like extra work in a culture that treats the home as a private refuge from others, rather than a place of discipleship and ministry.

So here are three things you can do today to begin cultivating this principle.

1. *Pick a Rhythm and Keep It*

Choose a church holiday, a saint's feast day, or one evening each month that you commit to hosting. Thursday Night Dinners are unique, and they're not possible for most people to replicate. So start where you are. Aside from weekly hosting, we celebrate Saint Michael and All Angels every year on September 29. It's one of our favorite times of the year. After researching traditional foods and the story behind the feast, we craft an evening liturgy of food, fellowship, and worship. We serve a four-course meal including autumn salad and rolls, butternut squash soup, goose with bacon collards and carrots, and angel food cake. Between courses, friends read poems, Bible passages, or prayers that remind us of God's victory over the fallen angel, Satan. We also write letters of thanks to our local police officers, since Saint Michael is their patron. The goal is simple: bless those who come, bless our community, and anchor our own hearts in grateful worship.

2. Find a Hosting Friend

Build a small circle of people who want to be intentional about opening their homes. Hospitality grows best in community. Take turns hosting, share ingredients, and trade recipes. Some of the most meaningful moments come not from planned events but from small, last-minute acts of hospitality toward a friend whose power went out, a neighbor grieving, a family with a sick child, or in making time to listen and delight in a friend. Indeed, this is why true hospitality requires us to budget our time and attention.

A friend of mine, Ellie, keeps an extra lasagna in her freezer "just in case." Twice, it has ended up on a doorstep the same night she prayed for someone in need. That's the kind of readiness we're called to cultivate.

3. Use Your Table for Godly Influence

A woman can and will have untold reach through her table. Use it to strengthen your relationships with fellow friends, pastors, or colleagues. Invite those who you might never cross paths with otherwise. Resolve tension over coffee rather than email. Rebuild trust over a meal. Some of my favorite stories began with introducing two people who later built friendships, or even marriages.

Hospitality lowers defenses. It turns strangers into family and, like Esther, creates a space where truth can be spoken with grace. A shared table has the power to reconcile, to deepen friendships, and to confront evil.

Conclusion

As more women choose stay-at-home motherhood, build home-based work, or step away from the exhaustion of "girl-boss" culture, they are making a powerful decision to make room for God-given and God-commanded hospitality, beginning with their own families.

God is raising up a generation of women who remember. What many of us lost in childhood can be recovered again. That remembrance begins and ends at the table, and most often at our own tables at home. It is there that the stories of God's faithfulness—to our families and to our nation—are told and retold. The table is where Lady Wisdom presides and where our own wisdom is formed through the simple act of remembering. The psalmist prays, "So teach us to number our days that we may get a heart of wisdom" (Psalm 90:12).

Hospitality is not a side note in the life of a woman of God. It is not a hobby or a bonus for those with extra time. It is one of the most feminine, strategic, and meaningful ways to wield influence in our churches, communities, and even in our culture. It is costly and worth making hard sacrifices for, including a consideration of if our current work commitments are keeping us from wielding the kind of hospitality the Bible commands.

Life brings seasons of limitation, whether it's demanding jobs, illness, or financial strain. Still, whatever the season, simplicity, or form, the call remains the same: to be a Christian is to show God's hospitality to others. We host because God first hosted us.

Every time you lay out a meal and invite someone in, even just one person, you are fighting back against the kingdom of loneliness, the reign of passive acceptance, and the empire of *I'm fine.* Like Esther, whose carefully prepared table became the setting for justice and deliverance, your table, too, can be a place where God's purposes unfold.

Start where you are. You may not feel like a warrior. But when you brew coffee and listen well, you are dismantling despair. When you serve soup to someone who didn't expect kindness, you are toppling towers of shame. When you make a simple meal and speak blessing over your children, you are driving back generational curses.

Make the chili. Light the candle. Set one more place. Look your guest—your child, your neighbor, or your lonely friend—in the eye and say, *you are welcome here.* Because in a world that feasts on fear and isolation, a woman who feeds with love is a holy terror to the dark. So, take up your ladle like a sword. Stand behind your stove like a sentinel. Set your table like an altar.

PRINCIPLE FIVE

Marriage on Mission

Then the man said, "This at last is bone of my bones and flesh of my flesh; she shall be called Woman, because she was taken out of Man."

—Genesis 2:23

Every worldview has its own origin story, and Barbie and Ken are no different. In Greta Gerwig's 2023 film *Barbie*, she retells the story of Ruth Handler's famous doll. The film, which earned $155 million on its opening weekend, begins with a proactive image: a little girl smashing her baby dolls and choosing Barbie instead. This scene introduces Barbie as a symbol of possibility, created to help girls imagine themselves as anything they want to be. Barbie and Ken may live in a world of plastic perfection, and yet, the movie quickly shows us that they have forgotten their purpose. Gerwig's film sparked reactions across the spectrum, from transgender activists to social conservatives, each claiming it supported their worldview. Whether or not my interpretation is entirely correct, I see the film as one of the most compelling reflections on the ongoing battle between the sexes.

Hollywood's creation story shifts between two incomplete examples of marriage and the relationship between the sexes. On the one hand, author and psychologist Joseph Campbell gives us *The Hero with a Thousand Faces,* naming the natural arc of a hero's journey in mythology.[1] His account shaped countless stories from *Star Wars* to *The Matrix*. But Campbell's journey is fundamentally male. It only tells one side of the story. When his student Maureen Murdock asked, "What about the women?" Campbell famously replied to Murdock, saying, "Women don't need to make the journey. In the whole mythological tradition the woman is there. All she has to do is to realize that she's the place that people are trying to get to."[2] While women may serve as guides or motivators, they tend to be a steady, even static, characters.

But Maureen Murdock wasn't satisfied. She wrote *The Heroine's Journey* in response, trying to carve out a distinctly female path.[3] But instead of letting the rich tradition of biblical and mythological women speak for themselves, her 1990 book tends to reflect the post-1960s feminist ideals that apply male norms to women. The result is a pseudo-masculine character inside a woman's body.

In Murdock's journey, the first step is a woman's rejection of the feminine. She casts aside motherhood and homemaking to embrace a masculine world. Along the way, she undergoes internal trials and successes, eventually "healing the mother/daughter split," "healing the wounded masculine," and achieving the "integration of the masculine and feminine" in herself. Campbell's hero's journey may be incomplete for women, but Murdock's is, too. Murdock wants to create a whole person but ends up only making an asexual person with no husband, no children, and ultimately, no meaningful connection to the opposite sex. Unlike Campbell's hero, who needs the woman to complete his journey, Murdock's heroine stands alone.[4]

This brings us back to the movie *Barbie*. More than any film in recent memory, *Barbie* shows the limitations of both Campbell's and Murdock's narratives by telling two journeys side by side: Barbie's and Ken's.

Barbie Land is a world ruled by women. They are presidents, Supreme Court justices, construction workers—everything. Men, by contrast, are accessories. This world is also plastic, superficial, and sterile. No one grows up, falls in love, or has children. The characters even joke that beneath their clothes, they have only smooth, plastic mounds. (Notably, the "transgender Barbie" exists only in Barbie Land, and not the real world.)

Their perfect world begins to crumble when Barbie starts questioning the purpose of life as cellulite, thoughts of death, and flat feet plague her. To figure out what is going on, she journeys into the real world. Here, she discovers that womanhood involves pain, aging, sacrifice, but also profound beauty. In the end, Barbie chooses to become a real woman. The film closes with her comically earnest first visit to a gynecologist, leaving viewers to decide whether this moment celebrates reproductive autonomy as a natural right or affirms biology as central to being a woman.

And yet, something's missing. Or rather, *someone*.

At the end, Ken confesses, "I don't know who I am without you." Barbie answers, "You're Ken." He protests, "But it's Barbie *and* Ken." After rejecting his romantic advances, Barbie replies, "You have to figure who you are without me." Barbie tells Ken to find himself without her. In doing so, she repeats Murdock's core mistake that we can fully know what it means to be a man or a woman apart from the opposite sex.

Barbie's advice misses a radical truth: that men and women *together* reflect the *imago Dei*. Whether it is through marriage, family, or friendships as brothers and sisters in Christ, neither man nor woman can fully understand their calling and purpose in the world without the other. Only in relation to one another do they reflect the full image of God in the world.

That is why our fifth principle is marriage on mission, which restores husbands and wives as battle-mates rather than rivals or isolated individuals. It calls them to embrace a shared mission to build God's kingdom together in the home, the church, and the community.

Overcoming the Battle of the Sexes as Battle-Mates

We can learn a lot about our purpose and calling in the world by looking back at our own origin story, as told in Genesis 1 and 2. As Psalm 100:3 declares, "Know that the Lord, he is God! It is he who made us, and we are his; we are his people, and the sheep of his pasture." The God who created us is the one who gives us our purpose and defines our limitations. So, if we want to understand what it means to be a man and woman today, we must start with God's own Word.

This is a great relief for me as an author, and as a recipient. As an author, it takes undo pressure off. I'm not here to write a marriage book (I have only been married for a few years as it is!) but to share some of my observations about the fullness of God's Word to husbands and wives, men and women. God's Word is active, sharper than any two-edged sword (Hebrews 4:12), so I am grateful that you'll join me on this exploration of our origin story, and a few great and not-so-great-marriages in the Bible.

I have worked full-time since Jack and I got married and began having children. A lot of women talk about the pressures of trying to work and care for children (something I will dive into fully in the next chapter), but what no one prepared me for was how difficult it is to fully support my husband with both of us working two different jobs full-time. For me, the deeper tension wasn't motherhood versus work, but work versus being a fully present wife. We weren't distant emotionally, but it felt like we were two trains running side-by-side. It wasn't a lack of desire to submit or follow his lead, but more like a lack of a shared vision and understanding of how to accomplish it.

That unfulfilled ache and desire for understanding takes us all the way back to Genesis 1 and 2. Genesis 1, the chapter on the creation of the world, reaches it high point when God creates man and woman.

> Then God said, "Let us make man in our image, after our likeness. And let them have dominion over the fish of the sea and over the birds of the heavens and over the livestock and over all the earth and over every creeping thing that creeps on the earth."
>
> So God created man in his own image, in the image of God he created him; male and female he created them.
>
> And God blessed them. And God said to them, "Be fruitful and multiply and fill the earth and subdue it, and have dominion over the fish of the sea and over the birds of the heavens and over every living thing that moves on the earth." (Genesis 1:26–28)

Here the Bible emphasizes the creation of man and woman and their calling as human beings—regardless of if they ever got married or not. This is the "big picture" description, if you will.

Then, in the very next chapter, the Bible retells the creation narrative. This time, however, it slows the story way down and focuses on the specifics, starting with Adam.

The Bible tells us that God formed Adam (whose name means "earth") from the dust of the ground and breathed the breath of life into his lungs. Then God says, "It is not good that the man should be alone; I will make him a helper fit for him" (Genesis 2:18). This is the first time that God says something is *not good*, and it occurs without the presence of sin. It is not an admission of wrongdoing on God's part, nor a reference to Adam feeling sad or lonely. God wanted to open Adam's eyes so that he could see that unlike the animals, he didn't have a "a helper fit for him." Adam was incomplete. Adam could not reflect God in God's fullness alone.

Translated from the Hebrew, that phrase is *ezer kenegdo*. As theologian Peter Leithart writes in *The Glory of Man*, the English word "helper" has been sadly domesticated.[5] It conjures images of assistants or sidekicks, perhaps someone who "helps around the house."[6] In the Bible, however, *ezer* is used almost exclusively in military or political contexts. It describes someone who brings strength to another—most often, God Himself (see Psalm 33:20 and Deuteronomy 33:7).

As Leithart puts it,

> A helper puts himself at the service of the helped, but *ezer* doesn't necessarily imply permanent subordination or essential inferiority. Some helpers are subordinates (David's mighty men), some are superiors (Yahweh). *Ezer* doesn't imply weakness. On the contrary, a helper must be strong in order to help, and the weakness, if any, is on the side of the one who *needs* help.[7]

Leithart describes how the second half of the phrase, *kenegdo*, combines two Hebrew prepositions: *k*- ("like") and *neged* ("in front of," or "opposite"). "The combination yields a paradox: Adam's helper will be 'like opposite him.' The *ezer* will be like him in ways animals are not, yet so different as to be opposed."[8] She is his mirror, his counterpart, and his challenger—understood as iron sharpening iron and a playful and respectful dialogue (Proverbs 27:17).

This is what it means to be a *battle-mate.*[9]

And so, God offers Adam as the first living sacrifice to bring forth woman from his side. As minister Matthew Henry famously wrote, "The woman was made of a rib out of the side of Adam; not made out of his head to rule over him, nor out of his feet to be trampled upon by him, but out of his side to be equal with him, under his arm to be protected, and near his heart to be beloved."[10]

Strictly speaking, Adam never finds the promised *ezer kenegdo.* Waking up from his slumber, Adam rapturously speaks the first poem, filled with awe and love. "This at last is bone of my bones and flesh of my flesh; she shall be called Woman because she was taken out of Man" (Genesis 2:23). Can you hear the overwhelming relief in his voice? Can you feel the delight with which he beheld her?

Adam, whose name reflects his origin from the earth, does not call the woman his *ezer,* but *ishshah,* a play on words meaning "fire" or "burning." In naming the woman, the man also renames himself in relation to her as *ish* (man). In Eve, Adam encounter's identity and difference. And it is exactly what he, and Eve, need to fully embody and reflect God's image.

But the Bible, and Peter Leithart, don't stop there. To summarize Leithart, both the man and the woman are given two names that show where they come from and what they are meant to do.[11]

The man is called Adam, linked to the *adamah* (earth), showing his origin and his task to work the ground, and he is also called *ish*, connected to *ishshah* (woman), showing his bond with her. The woman is called *ishshah*, since she comes from *ish* (man), and later *chawwah* or Eve, meaning "mother," highlighting her role in bearing children.[12]

These names reveal that each is pulled in two directions: the man is drawn both to the earth and to the woman, while the woman is drawn both to the man and to her children. This tension—between their work and their relationships—is part of their design from the very beginning, even before the fall.

Adam is primarily responsible for work outside of the family as the protector and provider. Eve is primarily responsible for the cultivation of her home: her husband and children. This distinction in Genesis isn't meant to divide them but to clarify their priorities. Taken together, it outlines a vision for marriage where Adam and Eve are united in purpose and equipped to fulfill the creation mandate given in Genesis 1:26–28, working together to carry out God's plan.

It doesn't mean that Adam does not engage with his children—far from it! It is a wonderful blessing that men are far more involved in the day-to-day lives of their homes and children than in previous generations, and it mirrors Paul's vision of headship where husbands are primarily responsible for the spiritual formation and maturity of their families (1 Timothy 3:1–7).

Similarly, it does not mean that Eve cannot work outside the home. She, as Paul directs, must be the keeper of her home (Titus 2:5) first and foremost, discerning carefully what she takes on in addition to that. In this way, Adam and Eve's two names help us understand our origin story and our primary calling, too.

It is after the fall that this natural relationship to the world and to each other becomes broken and corrupt. To summarize an analogy used by author and speaker Rosaria Butterfield during the Center for Christian Virtue Essential Summit I attended earlier this year, Eve, and all women after her, will wage war against her progeny and the patriarchy (Genesis 3:16).[13] Likewise, Adam, and all men after him, will work the land that he was created from in hardship and frustration until they eventually return to it in death. For both Adam and Eve, sin ruins their God-given calling to be fruitful. What was meant to be a delight-filled labor, receiving God's good gifts from fertile ground, is now marked by pain and hardship.

Adam began Genesis 2 looking for his *ezer*, and by the time we get to Genesis 3, God promises Adam a *zera* (seed) who will crush sin and death once and for all.

Even though sin distorts God's original design, it does not erase it. The calling of man and woman to be fruitful and multiply continues, but now it must be carried out in a world marked by conflict, frustration, and the need for redemption. In this context, the Bible shows us how hierarchy and mutuality come together in God's plan for marriage.

As Leithart beautifully summarizes, "In light of the rest of Scripture, we know there's a hierarchy in marriage; the husband is the head, the woman the body, and the wife submits to the husband as to Christ (Ephesians 5:22–23)."[14] Husbands, also, lay down their lives for their wives and men rely on women for their birth. He continues, "But she submits as a queen to a king, a lieutenant to a general. Her primary field of combat may be the home, but the woman isn't created to be a servant or a domestic helper. She's created to join the man as his compatible battle-mate who stands at his shoulder to fight his adversaries."[15]

If Barbie and Ken had embraced this vision, their story could have ended very differently. Instead of going their separate ways, Ken could have stepped into his calling to lead with strength and humility, using his position to serve and protect Barbie. She could have received that leadership as a gift and brought her own gifts alongside his, shaping their life together with wisdom and care. Their relationship would have been marked by purpose, reflecting the picture of Christ and the church where love orders and directs their shared mission.

Even in the film, the first real innovation in Barbie Land happens after Ken returns with the idea of patriarchy and begins to lead. While Gerwig presents it as messy and misguided, it shows the strength of male leadership. While women tend to lean toward stability, strong and godly men propel society forward. One isn't better than the other; both are essential. If they had embraced a rightly ordered vision, that movement could have been directed toward lasting good. Together, they could have returned to Barbie Land with a united purpose. Ken's leadership would have provided stability and direction, while Barbie's creativity and nurturing would have brought life and beauty to what they were building. Their differences would no longer divide them but drive them forward, each sharpening and strengthening the other. Side by side, they could have transformed their world into a place that reflected the fullness of God's image.

Finding an "Excellent Wife": The Story of Ruth and Boaz

One of the clearest and most redemptive examples of the battle-mate dynamic in the Bible appears in the book of Ruth. Ruth, a Moabite woman, married one of Naomi's sons after Naomi's family fled Israel during a famine. In a tragic turn of events, Naomi's husband and both of her sons died, leaving her destitute and alone in a foreign land—a place where Israelites were not meant to settle, much less intermarry.

When Naomi heard the famine in Israel had ended, she decided to return home. Ruth and Orpah, her daughters-in-law, began the journey with her, but Naomi urged them to go back to their own families rather than face an uncertain future in a foreign land. Orpah eventually turned back, but Ruth refused. Her words remain among the most powerful examples of covenantal loyalty in the Bible: "For where you go I will go, and where you lodge I will lodge. Your people shall be my people, and your God my God" (Ruth 1:16).

In Israel, Ruth humbly placed herself under Naomi's care, relying on her wisdom to guide the way. Like Esther listening to Mordecai, Ruth leaned on the wisdom of one who knew more than she did. Naomi instructed Ruth to glean in the fields of Boaz, a near relative and prominent landowner. Ruth obeyed. Her diligence and humility caught Boaz's attention, and he instructed his workers to leave behind extra grain for her.

As Naomi continued to guide her, she developed a plan to secure Ruth's future by positioning her before Boaz as a potential wife. Boaz, as a close relative, held the legal right to redeem their family line through marriage. Naomi's plan was bold, even risky: she instructed Ruth to go to Boaz under the cover of night and uncover his "feet" as he slept—a term that in Hebrew (*regel*) can serve as literal and euphemistic. Either way, Ruth's actions pressed the point: Boaz needed to step up and redeem her or stop wasting her time. Naomi was not about to enable a "situationship."

By approaching Boaz in such a vulnerable way, Ruth took a real risk. He could have humiliated her or taken advantage of her sexually without making any commitments. Instead, just as Naomi believed he would, Boaz showed integrity. He protected Ruth's dignity, sent her home with provisions, and promised to settle the matter publicly by seeking to fulfill his role as redeemer.

Throughout the book, the Bible describes Ruth (3:11) using the Hebrew word *ḥayil*—translated as "excellent," "valiant," or "worthy." This same word describes Boaz in Ruth 2:1, and their union in 4:11. While often translated as "excellent wife/woman," *ḥayil* fundamentally means strength: military strength, moral strength, wealth, or valor. It is used to describe David's warriors and God's own actions on behalf of His people.

Ruth was *ḥayil* before she married Boaz. Boaz, likewise, was *ḥayil* before he met Ruth. Their union didn't make them virtuous; it revealed and strengthened the virtue already within them. And together, they embodied a fruitful *hayil* bearing children and good works from their union.

Interestingly, the Bible rarely uses *ḥayil* to describe women in the Old Testament. Aside from Ruth, the only other notable example comes from the Proverbs 31 "woman of valor."

By following a godly woman, Ruth became one. Many Jewish traditions see Ruth as the inspiration behind the Proverbs 31 "excellent wife," which makes sense. As Solomon's great-great-grandmother, Ruth embodied the courageous, diligent, and wise femininity described in Proverbs. What does this excellent woman look like? Solomon offers a list that sounds remarkably like Ruth herself:

- Her husband trusts her completely, and she adds value to his life.
- She works for the good of her family, home, and community every day.
- She takes initiative and works with skill, handling the daily needs of her household.

- She shops wisely and seeks out quality, bringing home the best she can find.
- She wakes early, manages her time well, and provides for those in her care.
- She makes smart decisions about money and opportunities, even investing and buying property.
- She is strong, capable, and ready to meet the demands of her work.
- She builds and creates, turning raw materials into useful and valuable products.
- She shares what she has, caring generously for the poor and vulnerable.
- She plans ahead, prepares for hard seasons, and keeps her family safe and secure.
- She runs a productive household, managing resources wisely and supporting her husband's work.
- She uses her words to teach, guide, and encourage with wisdom and kindness.
- Her children respect and honor her, and her husband openly praises her: "Many women have done excellently, but you surpass them all."
- She knows that although physical beauty fades, the fear of the Lord is her strength.
- Her work speaks for itself, and her faithfulness is recognized by those around her.

Proverbs 31 isn't here to burden women with impossible standards or make them feel inadequate. Illustrated by Ruth's own life, it offers a clear and compelling vision for wise and capable women to build, nurture, lead, and serve with strength and faithfulness. Beginning with the fear of the Lord, it's an invitation to grow into that kind of woman, step by step, wherever God has placed us.

The Tent Peg Strategy: Application

Taken together, these examples make one thing unmistakably clear: men and women rise or fall together. The battle of the sexes leads only to mutual destruction. We need one another as we walk in wisdom and live out God's good design for men, women, and marriage. With that in mind, we can now turn to five practical ways to live this out today.

1. Don't Awaken Love Before Its Time

Three times in the Song of Solomon, the author pleads with the daughters of Jerusalem "not to stir up or awaken love until it pleases" (Song of Solomon 2:7; 3:5; 8:4). That repeated warning carries timeless wisdom. Love flourishes best in the right season, when both people are ready to pursue it with purpose and clarity. Sliding into emotional intimacy before that time often leads to confusion, disappointment, and misplaced expectations.

Modern dating culture makes this harder than ever. Many relationships today begin online, through apps, text messages, social media, or endless DM conversations. Because of that, it is easy to build a sense of closeness without really knowing a person at all. Emotional bonds form quickly, often without any real intention to pursue a relationship or any meaningful knowledge of the other person's character, habits, family, or faith. The result is a growing epidemic of "situationships"—relationships defined by emotional vulnerability but lacking clarity, commitment, or direction.

As followers of Christ, we are called to guard our hearts and the hearts of others. That means setting wise boundaries around how close we allow ourselves to become with someone before a relationship is clearly defined. If emotional depth is growing but commitment is not, that is a sign that something is off. Like Boaz and Ruth, we should bring intentions into the light rather than lingering in confusion. Ruth made her intentions clear, and Boaz responded by acting decisively and honorably. We should do the same.

One practical way to guard your heart is to ask yourself an honest question: Would I have this same level of closeness, conversation, and vulnerability with this person if I were married or seriously dating someone else? If the answer is no, then it is time to set a boundary. Friendship between men and women is possible in the casual, social sense, but deep emotional intimacy almost always carries the possibility of romance, whether we admit it or not. There is even research to back this up. In 1997, psychologists Arthur Aron and Elaine N. Aron conducted a study in which pairs of strangers answered a series of thirty-six increasingly personal questions and then spent four minutes gazing into one another's eyes.[16] The researchers found that "sustained, escalating, reciprocal, personal self-disclosure" consistently produced closeness, and in several cases, the participants went on to form serious relationships and even marry. The lesson is simple and sobering: growing degrees of emotional intimacy have a powerful pull, and over time they can draw two people toward romantic attachment, even if neither intended it from the start.

This pattern is easy to spot in our culture today. In the movie *Made of Honor*, Patrick Dempsey's character, Tom, spends years being "just friends" with Hannah, his closest confidant. He dates other women and keeps things casual, but their bond deepens over time. Everything changes when Hannah gets engaged. Only then does Tom realize that their connection was never neutral. Their friendship had always been charged with romantic potential, and once faced with losing her, he wants to pursue her.

Deep emotional bonds between men and women rarely stay neutral, and pretending they will is unwise. Waiting to awaken love protects the heart, clarifies intentions, and creates the right environment for a relationship to grow in the right time and way.

2. Be Good at Being a Woman, Not Just a Good Woman

There is a difference between being a good woman and being good at being a woman. Pursuing godliness, wisdom, and virtue is essential. That's the starting point. Every Christian woman is called to grow in character, to fear the Lord, and to reflect Christ in her words, work, and relationships. But if we stop there, we miss something important. God created womanhood as a unique and beautiful gift, and learning how to embody that gift is part of growing in practical wisdom.

Being good at being a woman means embracing and cultivating distinctly feminine strengths. It's about more than morality. It's about learning to carry yourself with grace, strength, and warmth—to present yourself as someone who is both dignified and approachable and to create a home that reflects beauty, order, and comfort. This will look different depending on your culture and personality, but the principle remains the same: femininity has an external expression, and it takes intentionality to develop it.

Start with the practical. Seek out godly older women who embody the qualities you hope to develop—women who dress and carry themselves well, who speak with confidence and kindness, who manage their homes with skill and care. Ask for their help and advice. Pay attention to the details: your health, your posture, your clothing, how you communicate, and how you manage your time. Learn how to style your hair, care for your skin, and present yourself in a way that reflects dignity and confidence. Stay active, not just for appearance but to cultivate discipline and self-control. These small habits matter. They reflect how you view yourself and the God who made you.

One of the greatest compliments I received during my engagement was when a friend said, "Emma, since getting serious with Jack, there's a warmth and softness in you that wasn't there before." That kind of softness is the sign of a woman who feels safe, protected, and well cared for when a godly man steps into their calling to lead, protect, and provide.

As the dedication of Megan Basham's book *Beside Every Successful Man* reads, "For Brian, who assures me that I could conquer the world and then tells me I don't have to."[17] It's the freedom to exhale, set down your burdens, and trust your husband or father to competently fight on your behalf.

Like Barbie and Ruth, women can cultivate feminine virtues on their own, but those virtues reach their fullest expression in the context of healthy relationships with strong, godly men—men who reflect the character of not just a good man, but a man who is good at being a man.

And just as women are called to grow in femininity, men are called to grow in masculinity. Many of us know godly men in our churches who love the Lord and walk with integrity, yet they lack the qualities that make them compelling and attractive *as men*. In the same way, our growth as women should aim beyond just being virtuous, though never less. We should grow in our ability to present ourselves and our homes with modesty and beauty, reflecting our own unique styles and tastes. That work prepares you to be the kind of battle-mate who not only walks faithfully with the Lord, but also strengthens, encourages, and complements the man who will lead you.

3. Learn How to Date

In many ways, one of the most hopeful developments I've seen in recent years is the rise of creative, community-based approaches to dating. Across denominations and traditions, mature Christian women are stepping in to help the next generation form lasting relationships. Some have launched small matchmaking networks that require recommendations from a pastor or trusted believer, deliberately pushing against the consumerist swipe culture that dating apps encourage. Others host regular swing dancing or salsa nights, creating spaces where men and women learn to relate to one another through healthy touch, playful interactions, and light-hearted environments. Still others use weddings as opportunities for matchmaking, thoughtfully pairing bridesmaids and groomsmen in the hope that new relationships might blossom.

These examples reflect something deeply biblical. In Ruth's story, we see a woman of *ḥayil* pursuing a man of *ḥayil*. Her life offers two simple but profound invitations. First, do not date in isolation. Seek out wise mentors, older couples, or pastors who can speak into your life, offer counsel, and even help make introductions. Second, focus more on your *posture* than pursuit. As a woman, position yourself wisely and attractively, but allow him to take the initiative.

This idea of posture is worth lingering on. Are you open to marriage, or are you guarded, distracted, and unavailable? Are you cultivating your own excellence so that you are becoming the kind of person you hope to marry? Are you embracing femininity? These are difficult questions to answer honestly, and this is precisely why the gentle insight of godly mentors is so valuable. They help us see what we cannot see in ourselves.

When Jack and I first started dating, one of the first things he did was buy a book called *How to Avoid Falling in Love with a Jerk: The Foolproof Way to Follow Your Heart Without Losing Your Mind* by John Van Epp. It offered practical, commonsense wisdom. As the author describes the book, we need to learn how to:

- Ask the right questions to inspire meaningful, revealing conversations with your partner.
- Judge character based on compatibility, relationship skills, friends, and patterns from family and previous relationships.
- Resolve your own emotional baggage so you're ready for a healthy relationship.[18]

Those are three healthy goals we should all have! It gave Jack a helpful framework for pursuing me thoughtfully and processing our relationship well. There are many resources like that—both Christian and secular—that teach us how to ask someone on a date, how to build a relationship with intentionality, and how to move toward marriage wisely.

This kind of practical knowledge is more needed than ever. Many young people today aren't going on dates, aren't learning how to playfully flirt, and seem paralyzed by fear or intimidation toward the opposite sex. The "battle of the sexes" has turned men and women into adversaries—on one side, there is fear of a "Me Too" accusation; on the other, there is disappointment over a lack of leadership, reliability, or courage. Dating should not feel like warfare. With strong discernment, boundaries, and the insight of parents, it should be a joyful, self-forgetful exploration of another person. That's what we need to learn how to foster today.

4. Redefine Success as a Joint Pursuit, Beginning with the Husband's Career

When we marry, our lives are no longer lived for ourselves alone. God weaves our stories together into a shared mission, and that mission calls us to use our gifts in ways that strengthen and advance one another's callings. As an *ezer*, a battle-mate, a wife plays a vital role in whether that shared work flourishes. Our presence, our wisdom, and our efforts either push the mission forward or hold it back. It is a sacred responsibility.

The pattern for this was set at the very beginning. In Genesis 2, God placed Adam in the garden with a vocation to cultivate and keep it. Eve was created as an *ezer kenegdo* to join him in that mission. The order matters. Adam received the calling first, and Eve was brought into that work as his counterpart and partner. There is a sense in which this calling is not mutual. The husband bears the primary responsibility to lead and to set the direction, while the wife is invited to join and submit to that calling. Yet a wise and godly husband does not simply drag his wife along behind him. He listens carefully to her strengths, gifts, and insights, and he seeks to incorporate them into the mission they share. His leadership makes room for her calling, and her calling strengthens and enriches his.

Part of that calling is to pour our strength into our husband's work so that he can flourish in what God has given him to do. In turn, that shared fruitfulness shapes our own purpose as well. When I married Jack, I knew that part of my role was to be a faithful wife and a partner in his vocation as a pastor. One of my friends made a similar decision. When her husband became a teaching elder, she cut back her work to about ten hours a week. She wanted to have the bandwidth to host people, counsel alongside him, and care for their children as his responsibilities increased. Others do this by serving beside their husbands in church or community work, or by shaping their own careers in ways that complement their husband's leadership.

A powerful picture of this kind of strength appears in the official 2025 White House portrait of First Lady Melania Trump. Photographed in black and white by Régine Mahaux, the portrait shows Mrs. Trump standing in the Yellow Oval Room, dressed in a sharp black tuxedo and a crisp white shirt, the open collar adding a hint of softness and vulnerability. Behind her, the Washington Monument rises in the background, a quiet symbol of national strength and historical continuity. Every detail in Mrs. Trump's portrait seems carefully chosen to send a clear, powerful message. Her perfectly manicured nails hint at her precision and polished demeanor. The minimalist makeup, defined brows, and Mona Lisa–like smile suggest that she has set aside her own personal feelings and emotions for a single-minded focus on a greater mission.

The Washington Monument in the background recalls the influence of women like Dolley Madison and Elizabeth Schuyler Hamilton, whose hospitality, social graces, and volunteerism were essential to the flourishing of the early republic. They worked tirelessly to preserve the legacy of America's great men and strategically influenced politics at the parties they hosted. As Catherine Allgor notes in *Parlor Politics: In which the Ladies of Washington Help Build a City and a Government*, "Power sharing and compromise—the requisites for an effective political culture—seemed inconceivable to the men who held office, but not to Dolley, who built coalitions and connections every week in her drawing rooms."[19]

Traditionally, first lady portraits are warm, traditionally feminine, and inviting—designed to soften the commanding presence of their husbands. Mrs. Trump's 2017 portrait fits that mold. While the president appeared stern in his first official portrait, she balanced him out, making him seem more approachable and relatable. And that dynamic is both good and effective. But her 2025 portrait tells a different story. It reflects a deeper, more refined vision of complementary strength shaped by years of political battles. In this image, she doesn't just support from the sidelines; she stands beside him as a true battle-mate.

5. Wise Wives Uplift Their Husbands and Stand Firm Against Foolishness or Abuse

The call to be a battle-mate is a high and holy one. It involves strengthening, encouraging, and honoring the man you have covenanted your life with. A wise wife speaks life into her husband. She uplifts him with her words and her prayers, encourages him in his leadership, and calls him toward the man God created him to be. She believes that strong, faithful men who protect, provide, and lay down their lives for others are essential to the flourishing of families, churches, and communities. That kind of leadership thrives in the soil of respect and encouragement.

That does not mean a wife is called to quietly endure sin, foolishness, or harm. Submission in the Bible is never blind allegiance. The Bible calls wives to submit to their husbands "as to the Lord," which means submission is always ordered under obedience to God's Word (Ephesians 5:22). It never asks a wife to condone abuse, participate in wrongdoing, or stand by when a foolish decision would harm their family.

The story of Abigail offers one of the clearest pictures in Scripture of wise and active submission. Married to Nabal, a wealthy but "harsh and badly behaved" man (1 Samuel 25:3), she found herself in the middle of a crisis that could have cost their household everything. David and his men had protected Nabal's shepherds in the wilderness, yet when David sent a respectful request for provisions, Nabal mocked him: "Who is David? Who is the son of Jesse?" (25:10). His arrogant refusal provoked David's anger, and he set out with four hundred men, determined to destroy Nabal's household.

When Abigail heard what had happened, she acted quickly and decisively. Without telling her husband, she gathered an abundant gift of food and rode out to meet David. As soon as she saw him, "she hurried and got down from the donkey and fell before David on her face" (1 Samuel 25:23). In humility, she took responsibility for the offense: "On me alone, my lord, be the guilt" (v. 24). But her words went far beyond apology. She appealed to David's conscience and to his calling, reminding him that the Lord Himself would establish his throne and urging him not to stain his future with unnecessary bloodshed. "And when the Lord has done to my lord according to all the good that he has spoken concerning you. . . my lord shall have no cause of grief or pangs of conscience for having shed blood without cause. . ." (25:30–31).

David listened. He recognized that God had sent Abigail to stop him from committing sin. "Blessed be the Lord, the God of Israel, who sent you this day to meet me! Blessed be your discretion, and blessed be you, who have kept me this day from bloodguilt" (1 Samuel 25:32–33). He accepted her gift, turned back from his plan, and sent her home in peace.

The next morning, when Nabal sobered, Abigail told him what she had done. His heart failed him, and ten days later "the Lord struck Nabal, and he died" (1 Samuel 25:38). David, deeply moved by Abigail's wisdom and courage, later asked her to become his wife.

Abigail's story shows that submission is never a call to passive silence. It is a posture of discernment, humility, and strength. She honored her husband's role but did not enable his sin. She protected her household, appealed to righteousness, and intervened for the sake of God's purposes. Her example reminds us to seek help from the right people: older, trusted women; church elders and pastors; and, when necessary, civil authorities. Submission does not mean isolation. It does not mean silently enduring financial recklessness, spiritual manipulation, or physical abuse. It also does not mean gossiping or tearing your husband down in casual conversations with peers. Godly counsel flows through the right channels and with the right motives.

We need more women like Abigail: women who speak with clarity, act with courage, and seek God's wisdom, especially when threats come from within. And we need them to act sooner, before foolishness hardens into destruction. Wise wives nurture, encourage, and honor their husbands, but they also guard their homes and their souls with holy resolve. This is what it means to be an *ezer*: a strong helper, a battlemate, and a woman who builds her house on the fear of the Lord.

Conclusion

God designed husbands to lead with courage, conviction, and sacrificial love—to lay down their lives for their wives and families, to protect, provide, and press forward when the world grows dark. In response, wives are called to offer strength through willing submission—the free and deliberate choice to come alongside their husband's leadership with wisdom, counsel, and loyalty. Together, their marriage becomes a force for good. Their differences sharpen and strengthen one another. Their shared vision multiplies their impact. And that mission does not stop with them. It continues as they welcome children, disciple them, and raise the next generation to stand firm on God's Word. In the next chapter, we will turn to motherhood itself: its dignity, its demands, and how women can practice wise, joyful stewardship in the season of bearing and raising children.

PRINCIPLE SIX

Motherhood as Warfare

Behold, children are a heritage from the LORD, *the fruit of the womb a reward. Like arrows in the hand of a warrior are the children of one's youth. Blessed is the man who fills his quiver with them! He shall not be put to shame when he speaks with his enemies in the gate.*

—Psalm 127:3–5

I still remember sitting in my Feminist Theology class during my sophomore year in college, feeling both curious and unsettled. The themes were familiar: critiques of patriarchy, frustration with male-dominated biblical exegesis, and concern about the underrepresentation of women in church leadership. As the semester went on, I grew disillusioned. The class often defined womanhood by grievances, some legitimate and many less so, and held up the adoption of male norms as the solution.

That framework soon felt fruitless. I began to ask a different question that became foundational in my personal and theological journey: What can women do that men cannot? The answer was obvious and profound. Women can bear children. I never believed a woman's identity should be reduced to childbearing. Yet in a world where ideology and technology attempt to erase the distinctions between male and female, childbearing stood out as one of the few irreducible differences that helped me make sense of what it means to be a woman.

I had always been pro-life. I loved children. I babysat, volunteered, and admired the beauty of family life. Still, when I pictured having children of my own, fear took over. I was ambitious, independent, and driven; my father's work ethic burned in my bones. Motherhood felt like a big wet baby blanket. I had long, emotional conversations with professors and mentors as I tried to face these fears. Why did it feel like everything I had worked for would collapse at the thought of motherhood?

Instead of beginning with the Bible, I began with myself. My first response flowed from fear: fear of losing myself, of losing time and opportunities, and even of losing my body. I wanted to control everything. I wanted to time children precisely, to decide how many, and to make sure they fit neatly inside my plan. It turns out I was not alone.

For every article that celebrates the goodness of children, it seems there are ten that caution against their cost in money, time, energy, and even meaning.

- Women liberated from the "burden" of family life
- Children as economic liabilities
- Motherhood as a roadblock to self-fulfillment
- A climate too fragile, a culture too unjust, and a career too demanding for parenting
- And still other accounts of motherhood that felt silly, sentimental, or purely focused on consumer choice: Pampers or Huggies?[1]

Recent studies reflect this mood. One study of Michigan residents in 2023 found that one-in-five had no desire to have children.[2] Another survey by the Harris Poll (2022) found that finances, work-life balance, housing costs, and climate change were all deterrents to a person's desire to have children, with the desire to maintain personal independence as the leading cause.[3] Personal, not external, factors carried the most weight.[4]

An NBC study of Generation Z voters in the 2024 election reported that among women who voted for Kamala Harris, marriage and children ranked near the bottom of thirteen priorities, with career at the top.[5] Among women who voted for Donald Trump, the pattern looked similar, with career listed second and marriage and motherhood appearing two-thirds down the list. Men who voted for Trump differed from the other groups by listing having children as a top priority.

This isn't just a young person's problem. In 2024, the US birth rate fell to an all-time low of 1.6 children per woman on average, far below the replacement rate of 2.1.[6] The replacement rate refers to the estimated number of children each woman needs to have, on average, to sustain current population levels. From Elon Musk to Health and Human Services Secretary Robert F. Kennedy Jr., many leaders have identified declining birth rates as a national security threat that requires a government response.[7] The economy, gross domestic product (GDP), Social Security, military readiness, K–12 and higher education systems, and eldercare all rely on new generations of children. While many demographers and family-policy experts sounded the alarm, others responded with indifference or defiance. As Monica Hesse wrote in the *Washington Post*, "A lot of women don't want 2.1 kids. We need an economic model in which that's okay."[8] Her call for a solution that does not involve an individual woman's "reproductive system" reflects the spirit of the age. After decades of abortion because of *Roe v. Wade* and girl-boss feminism that made women feel inferior for prioritizing marriage and children over a formal career, it is no surprise that mainstream women are skeptical. Even so, the answer is not to forgo childbearing or buy into an "ends justify the means" framework for why to have children. We need to recover motherhood altogether.

What we believe about children shapes how we receive them. When popular culture treats motherhood as a loss of time, money, body, or self, fewer women want to pursue it. Surveys show that women without children often imagine children very differently than women who have them, especially in the context of marriage. For instance, recent research reports that married parents register the highest levels of happiness and purpose in life compared to their peers without children.[9] The lived reality of becoming a mother shifts the entire experience.

In an August 2024 report for the Institute for Family Studies, Jean Twenge, Jenet Erickson, Wendy Wang, and Brad Wilcox found that "Married mothers are also significantly more likely to be very happy than married women without children and unmarried women with children. The analyses presented in this report control for age, family income, and education, so these factors cannot be the reason for the differences. Married women are also more likely than unmarried women to say that life was enjoyable most or all of the time: 47% of married mothers and 43% of married childless women say life is enjoyable, compared to 40% of unmarried mothers and 34% of unmarried childless women."[10]

Despite many self-reported studies of actual married mothers reporting the joy and fulfillment that children bring, my Feminist Theology class and the culture at large focused on the liabilities of womanhood and motherhood. What was I missing? Moreover, if the Bible calls children a blessing (see Psalm 127:3–5; Psalm 128:3–4; Proverbs 17:6; Genesis 33:5; 1 Samuel 1:27; Matthew 19:14), why does our culture treat them like a burden?

My mentor at the time, Meagan, asked me a simple question that changed everything: "What if you are thinking about children all wrong?" That question sent me back to the Bible, and what I found surprised me. Throughout the Bible, God uses the bearing and raising of children to sanctify and strengthen His people. Motherhood is a path of surrender and trust rather than a project of control. In submitting to

God's design, we receive more than a family. By walking in obedience, we understand more about our role in His kingdom and receive courage for the good works set before us.

This is why our sixth principle is about becoming warrior mothers. In motherhood, women grow in influence and strength as they disciple, discipline, and launch children to follow God faithfully. This is a spiritual calling and a force for good in the world. The relationship between mothers and children, and the call to be open to life, does not rest on arguments about national strength, sentimental appeal, or personal fulfillment. Children are an inherent good. Through them we reflect God's fruitfulness, fulfill the creation mandate, and wage war against sin, death, and the devil. As I reflected on the ways women lead in the home and in public life, I saw how often it is children who shape our loves, our protections, and our causes. Motherhood is not a detour from leadership; it is one of the most powerful and enduring forms of it.

Sarah's Journey

Few women in the Bible capture the longing, joy, pain, and ultimate promises of motherhood more vividly than Sarai, eventually renamed Sarah, the wife of Abraham. Their story spans much of Genesis, tracing their journey from God's initial call in Genesis 12 to Sarah's death in chapter 25. When God first called Abram (later renamed Abraham), He promised to make him "into a great nation" (Genesis 12:2, CEB). Upon Abram's arrival in Canaan, God pledged, "To your offspring I will give this land" (12:7, CEB). He repeated the promise: "I will give you and your offspring forever all the land that you see. I will make your offspring like the dust of the earth" (13:15–16, CEB), and again, "Look at the sky and count the stars, if you are able to count them. Then he said to him, 'Your offspring will be that numerous'" (15:5, CEB).[11]

Yet there was one glaring problem: Abram was seventy-five and Sarai sixty-five when we first meet them. Despite these repeated promises, they remained childless. Even so, Abraham believed the Lord, "and it was counted to him as righteousness" (15:6, CEB).

As the years passed without a child, the weight of barrenness grew heavier. In desperation, Sarai gave her Egyptian servant Hagar to Abram as a wife, and Hagar bore a son, Ishmael. But instead of peace, this decision introduced sin and division into their family. Rather than trust God to fulfill His promise, Sarai and Abram reached for the fruit of Hagar's womb. Like Eve grasping for the fruit in Eden, their actions seemed good to the eyes but only led to sin, family fighting, and deep pain for Sarai—and everyone involved. Abram and Sarai broke the covenantal pattern of "one flesh" (Genesis 2:24, CEB) and suffered deeply for it.

Sarai's struggle points us back to Genesis 1–3 and the foundations of God's design. In Genesis 1:26–31, we learn three fundamental truths about what it means to be human. First, God created us and therefore holds ultimate authority over who we are and what we do. Second, He made us in His image, which means every human life carries inherent dignity from conception to death. Third, He blessed man and woman with a shared calling to "be fruitful and multiply." While this fruitfulness extends beyond childbearing to all forms of human creativity and stewardship, procreation lies at the heart of the cultural mandate. This does not mean every person will bear biological children, but it does mean that the potential for childbearing and the goodness of children are woven into the fabric of what it means to be human.

Sin, however, fractured God's good design. In Genesis 3, the entrance of sin broke humanity's relationship with God, with one another, and with the created world. The consequences of that fall appear in God's judgment on both Adam and Eve. To Eve He said, "I will surely multiply your pain in childbearing; in pain you shall bring forth children" (Genesis 3:16). The Hebrew word for "pain" here encompasses more than the physical pain of labor. It influences our desire to have or not have children, as well as the emotional, mental, and relational struggles that now accompany conception, pregnancy, childbirth, and childrearing. It also hints at a deeper temptation: the human impulse to idolize or attempt to control fertility itself.

Adam's curse mirrors this reality. In verse 17, God uses the same root word for "pain" to describe the toil and frustration Adam will face in his work, including the shared task of bringing forth life. Humanity's sinful desire for control over fruitfulness continued throughout Israel's history. When the people turned from worshiping God, they often turned to Baal and Asherah—false gods associated with fertility—in hopes that offering sacrifices or performing sexual acts in front of the statue would increase their crops or children. Across time, men and women alike have gone to great lengths, even beyond what is proper, in their attempts to fulfill or avoid the call to fruitfulness.

Sarai's own choices led to years of conflict. Hagar grew contemptuous of Sarai, Sarai responded harshly, Hagar fled, and God told her to return and submit, while also blessing her. Hagar even described God as "the God who sees me" (Genesis 16:13, NIV). Decades later, after Abraham's circumcision as a sign of the covenant, God reaffirmed His promise, renamed Sarai as Sarah, and promised that nations would come from her.

At that point, Abraham was one hundred and Sarah ninety, well past childbearing years. Abraham laughed at the promise, a deep, almost incredulous laugh (Genesis 17:15–17) and when three visitors—identified as "the Lord" in the text—confirmed the promise, Sarah laughed, too. "After I am worn out, and my lord is old, shall I have pleasure?" she wondered (Genesis 18:12). Yet God kept His word. Sarah gave birth to Isaac, whose name means "laughter," a testimony to God's faithfulness despite decades of waiting. Their story reminds us of Jesus's words in John 9:3 about the man born blind: "It was not that this man sinned, or his parents, but that the works of God might be displayed in him."

Sarah's story captures the entire spectrum of motherhood: deep desire, years of waiting, attempts at control, the joy of fulfillment, and fierce protection of her child. Her decision to use Hagar mirrors modern attempts to control fertility through surrogacy or reproductive technology, while her eventual delight in Isaac reveals the gift that comes from trusting God's timing.

Four Truths About God's Good Design for Children

Psalm 127 offers the clearest picture of what Sarah—and the rest of us—are called to embrace:

> Unless the Lord builds the house, those who build it labor in vain. Unless the Lord watches over the city, the watchman stays awake in vain. It is in vain that you rise up early and go late to rest, eating the bread of anxious toil; for he gives to his beloved sleep. Behold, children are a heritage from the Lord, the fruit of the womb a reward. Like arrows in the hand of a warrior are the children of one's youth. Blessed is the man who fills his quiver with them! He shall not be put to shame when he speaks with his enemies in the gate. (Psalm 127:1–5)

This psalm shows us four key truths.

1. Unless the Lord Builds the House

First, "Unless the Lord builds the house" teaches that God is the foundation of the family. He establishes the home, and apart from Him, all our efforts—no matter how noble—will fail. This verse anchors everything that follows. It reminds us that God alone is the architect of the family.

He is the builder, the designer, and the sustainer of the home. The psalmist is not speaking about brick and mortar but about the living, breathing household that grows from covenant love and shared obedience. Every part of family life, including marriage, parenting, discipleship, and mission, depends on His initiative and grace. And because the family was God's good idea, He defines its boundaries as marriage between one man and one woman, children through the sacred union of marriage or legitimate adoption, the godly submission of wife to husband and husband to Jesus Christ, and a delight in the three-fold purpose of marriage—for children, for comfort, and for godliness.

This truth confronts a deeply ingrained cultural impulse. We often believe that if we read enough books, implement the right routines, enroll our children in the best schools, and plan carefully for the future, we can build a thriving family by our own strength. But the Bible teaches that apart from God, all our efforts amount to nothing. A joyful marriage, wise and faithful children, and a home rooted in purpose cannot be engineered by strategy alone. They are the fruit of God's active presence.

2. *Children Are a Heritage from the Lord*

Second, "children are a heritage from the Lord" reminds us that they are gifts to be received with gratitude, not burdens to be managed or entitlements to demand. Even when children are unexpected, unwanted, or unhealthy, they are still gifts from God, worthy of our joyful acceptance and stewardship.

The psalmist begins with delight before giving any practical argument for children. He invites us to see their inherent goodness, to feel the warmth of a baby's giggle or the wonder of a child discovering the world. Children are not only valuable because of what they can do but because of who they are as beloved image-bearers of God. Many modern conversations about birthrates fail precisely because they treat children as a means to an end, whether to stabilize the economy or sustain social programs. Children are good in and of themselves, yet they are not a dead end.

To receive children as a heritage is to accept both the joy of their presence and the weight of our responsibility. We are called to cherish them, nurture them, and steward their lives with wisdom, knowing that they are gifts entrusted to us for God's glory.

3. Arrows in the Hand of a Warrior

The third truth the psalmist offers is that children are "like arrows in the hand of a warrior." This image is rich with meaning. Arrows are not ornamental. They are tools for battle, crafted with care and launched with purpose. In the same way, children are entrusted to parents for a reason. They are not only a source of joy but also a sacred responsibility through which God advances His kingdom. Through the raising of children, He refines our character, builds His Church, and sends faithful disciples into the world to proclaim His name.

The phrase "mighty warrior" describes someone who is strong, steadfast, and victorious. Applied to motherhood, it captures the endurance and resilience required for the work of bearing and raising children. Pregnancy, childbirth, and the daily labor of nurturing life are not small tasks. They shape a woman's heart and soul, forming her into someone she could not become otherwise. Motherhood transforms us. It calls us to die to ourselves, to surrender comfort and control, and to grow in strength, wisdom, and love. This is why how we speak about motherhood matters. Our words shape how we value this calling and how we step into it.

And warriors do not shoot arrows aimlessly. They craft them deliberately, sharpen them, and launch them toward a specific target.

Growing up, my dad often took us arrowhead hunting in the fields of South Georgia, especially after a heavy rain when the artifacts surfaced more easily. Just like he did as a boy, we'd walk the fields searching for traces of the past—arrowheads, pottery shards, and stone tools. Some finds were obvious, while others were harder to identify. My dad, with his trained eye, would guide us: "See how this one is shaped? Notice the sharp point and the wider base? That tail helps it fit into the bow." Some arrowheads were whole, but many were broken. Either way, we had to learn their purpose to recognize them and to see the difference between a battered stone and a weapon crafted with precision. Arrowheads had to be shaped carefully. If they were warped or flawed, they couldn't fly straight or hit the mark.

The same is true of children.

As mighty mothers, we don't raise our children aimlessly. We shape them with intention. We form them in the Word of God. We refine and train them to know God, love Him, and walk in obedience. Sharpened, ready arrows don't happen by accident. Parents must disciple their children spiritually, emotionally, and practically. This takes time, presence, and patience.

Modern life often fights against this calling. The demands of full-time work outside the home, particularly in the early years, can pull mothers away from the slow, steady work of discipleship. Cultural narratives often tell us that motherhood should accommodate career ambitions rather than the other way around. And yet, this holy work of discipleship cannot be outsourced. No one else is tasked with this sacred work.

Arrows are useless without a target, and targets are useless without arrows. As mighty mothers, we aim our children toward a clear and ultimate goal: God and His glory. Along the way, we hold specific hopes for our children, too. We hope they grow into people who are wise, hardworking, and full of integrity. We want them to do well in school, discover passions that ignite their sense of wonder, build strong marriages, raise families, and live with purpose. All these hopes serve one greater aim: to form children who love and glorify God with their whole lives.

4. Blessed Is the Man [and Woman] Who Fills His Quiver with Them

Finally, after tracing God's covenant promises, the goodness of children, and their purpose in His redemptive plan, the psalmist concludes with a blessing: "Blessed is the man who fills his quiver with them! He shall not be put to shame when he speaks with his enemies in the gate" (Psalm 127:5). This is not a call to have a particular number of children, nor is it an endorsement of movements that have distorted this passage into a legalistic mandate. Instead, the psalmist is showing us something far deeper: children are a public testimony and witness. They are living examples of God's goodness to us, and they are a visible reflection of whether parents are producing good or bad fruit.

In the ancient world, the "gate" was the center of public life, the place where elders gathered to make decisions, settle disputes, and conduct legal matters. To have many children standing with you there was a mark of honor and strength. It meant that your life's work extended beyond yourself. It meant that your family stood as a witness to God's goodness and faithfulness. In the same way today, children remain one of the clearest legacies a person can leave. They outlast our careers, reputations, and accomplishments. They embody what we taught and treasured.

If we're seeking wisdom—true wisdom rooted in the fear of the Lord—we must take seriously what God says about marriage, motherhood, and femininity. And here, once again, the psalmist declares that children are good. They are a blessing. Blessings are not always easy. They stretch us, refine us, and change us for the better. They give us what we didn't have before. Children do exactly that.

Isaiah affirms this truth when he describes children as "signs and symbols" of God's greater work (Isaiah 8:18). Throughout the Bible, the births and names of children often carry prophetic meaning, pointing to God's judgment, His salvation, or His promises for the future. Their very existence tells a story about who God is and what He is doing in the world. That is still true today. When people welcome children, they declare hope in God's future and trust in His provision. When a culture turns away from bearing and raising children, it reveals something about its spiritual condition—its fears, its priorities, and its belief about what is worth investing in.

Children, then, are not only a private joy but also a public witness. They are a means by which women and men alike participate in God's mission, contend against evil, and testify to His goodness. Through them, we fight the battle of faith in our homes and in the world. They are the legacy we leave behind and the living testimony that God's promises are still unfolding from one generation to the next.

From the New Testament, Back to Sarah, and to Us Today

Paul captures the redemptive thread in 1 Timothy 2:15: "Yet she will be saved through childbearing—if they continue in faith and love and holiness, with self-control." Though often misunderstood, this passage points to the salvation of the world through the birth of Christ. Mary's obedience stands in contrast to Sarah's doubt. Like Sarah, Mary's circumstances seemed impossible, but she trusted God's word rather than taking control into her own hands. As "warrior mothers," we are called to a similar posture: to pursue marriage, remain open to life, and steward our fertility with wisdom. The Bible does not prescribe a specific number of children or say to have as many as is possible, but it does call us to trust God in every season, including the difficult journey of infertility.

Abraham and Sarah were the first couple recorded in the Bible to wrestle with infertility, but they were far from the last. Isaac and Rebekah, Jacob and Rachel, Elkanah and Hannah, and Zechariah and Elizabeth all walked the same difficult road. Sarah's life, marked by a closed womb and the first recorded cave burial, is beautifully answered in the New Testament by the empty tomb and the new birth of Christ. Through Him, barrenness gives way to abundance, and death gives way to life. It is no accident, then, that the Apostle Peter holds up Sarah not merely as a wife but as an example of courageous faithfulness for all women. Writing to Christians scattered in exile, he says: "For this is how the holy women who hoped in God used to adorn themselves, by submitting to their own husbands, as Sarah obeyed Abraham, calling him lord. And you are her children, if you do good and do not fear anything that is frightening" (1 Peter 3:5–6).

This is a striking choice. Sarah's story is far from flawless. She doubted. She tried to control her circumstances. She took matters into her own hands with Hagar. Yet Peter still holds her up as a model for women today.

Peter's exhortation, "do not fear anything that is frightening," speaks to the heart of motherhood. Few callings expose our fears like this one. We fear whether we will conceive, whether our bodies will sustain life, whether we will have the strength to parent well. We fear for our children's safety, their futures, their faith, and their souls. We fear what we might lose, be it our time, our identity, or our ambitions. Fear creeps in at every stage, from the hope of pregnancy to the ache of an empty nest.

Peter knows this. The Greek word he uses for "frightening" is a rare military term that evokes the chaos of battle. He is not speaking about mild unease but about the kind of fear that rattles the soul and tempts us to retreat. In other words, he is preparing women to confront the real spiritual battle of motherhood. The stakes are high: motherhood is a holy calling, and Satan would love nothing more than to paralyze women with fear before they ever step into it—or tempt them to off-load it onto other people as they prioritize careers over the needs of children.

Sarah's story shows us another way. She walked into the unknown repeatedly, including leaving her homeland, traveling into foreign lands, enduring shame and disappointment, and waiting decades for God to fulfill His promise. She faced the deep fears of barrenness and the vulnerability of childbirth in old age. Yet she learned to trust God with what she could not control. Her story is not one of fragile timidity but of resilient courage.

Taken together, Sarah's story, the vision of Psalm 127, and Peter's charge to "do good and not fear anything that is frightening" form a single, sweeping picture of motherhood as God intends it to be. It is not a side project or a sentimental hobby. It is a central part of God's redemptive plan that stretches across generations, builds His kingdom, and wages war against the darkness.

On Work and Children

If the Bible calls children a "heritage from the Lord" and "arrows in the hand of a warrior," then it follows that how we care for them is not a secondary matter. It is one of the most sacred assignments entrusted to us. Discipling and forming our children is not simply an activity that fills our days; it is the heart of our vocation as women. And the more we understand how children are designed to grow and thrive, the clearer this truth becomes.

One of the most frustrating aspects of our cultural conversations about motherhood and work is that we often begin with the wrong question. We start by asking, "What is good for me?" rather than "What is good for my children and my marriage?" That shift in focus changes everything. The Bible is clear that our calling is to, first and foremost, lay down our lives for the next generation, to shape souls for eternity, and to prioritize their well-being above our own comfort, ambitions, or preferences.

Modern science confirms what the Bible has long taught about the deep, formative power of a mother's presence. As psychologist Erica Komisar explains, "Children are born neurologically fragile, not resilient, and certainly not capable of caring for themselves. The first three years of life are critical for social-emotional development, where a child needs the physical and emotional presence of their primary attachment figure—usually the mother—to buffer them from stress and regulate their emotions."[12] As Komisar goes on to explain, this period shapes the architecture of a child's brain and emotional life. During infancy, the brain is forming nearly one million new synapses every second, and most of that rapid growth is in the right hemisphere, which governs emotional regulation, social connection, and the capacity for empathy and intimacy.[13]

From the moment of birth, infants are primed to seek their mother's voice, smell, and touch.[14] They co-regulate their emotions through her presence.[15] A mother's soothing words, her gentle touch, her "motherese" tone of voice all work together to lower cortisol (the stress hormone), activate oxytocin (the bonding hormone), and establish a foundation for trust, emotional security, and future relationships.[16] This sacred attachment is not interchangeable. Fathers form their own crucial bonds with children, often influencing cognitive development and exploration, but the emotional core of security is first built in the mother's arms.[17]

When that bond is disrupted too soon or too often, the consequences are profound. According to a 2023 meta-analysis, nearly half (48.4 percent) of children show signs of insecure attachment, often rooted in early separation or inconsistent caregiving.[18] These attachment wounds can ripple into adulthood, shaping the way individuals form relationships, handle stress, and respond to intimacy. Children who lack a strong early attachment often struggle with emotional regulation, exhibit anxiety or aggression, and may repeat unhealthy relationship patterns later in life.[19] There is simply no replacement for a mother, especially in the early years of a child's life. It is cancelable offense to apply this to daycare and full-time out of the house work, and it is even worse to say that there is an added benefit, when possible, to have the mother home with them.[20]

Taken with the studies linked in the endnotes, the reality is that the total amount of time spent in childcare early in life can leave a lasting imprint on social and behavioral development, often continuing well beyond childhood. This results largely held true even when accounting for differences in family income, education, and quality of care at home.

The science of child development makes one truth impossible to ignore: there is no substitute for a mother's available and loving presence in the earliest years. Even the best daycare environments, with skilled and attentive caregivers, cannot replicate the bond forged between a mother and her child. Komisar puts it plainly: "Reducing mothers to a technical role, by equating them with day care workers, is not only false but harmful."[21] As Komisar goes on to describe, institutional care, particularly when introduced too early, often elevates cortisol levels, increasing stress and contributing to anxiety, aggression, and attachment disorders. Children forced to separate prematurely from their primary source of security may show signs of fear or detachment, seek comfort from indiscriminate adults, or display heightened aggression—all indications of disrupted attachment.[22]

For mothers, the brain tends to turn inward, tuning itself to the baby's inner world. Key parts of her brain become highly active, helping a mother detect even the tiniest flicker of her baby's feelings: a whimper of sadness, a sigh of contentment, or a burst of joy.[23] Other parts of the brain team up and weave those emotional signals into a story of what the child might be feeling or needing.[24] At the same time, reward centers light up, making every smile and coo feel deeply meaningful.[25] All of this neural activity nudges mothers toward soothing, nurturing, and comforting—behaviors that ask the question, "How is my baby feeling inside?"

Fathers' brains work a lot like mothers', but they often focus more on what's happening outside. The parts of the brain that help notice the surroundings, think ahead, and make plans become more active.[26] In other words, a father's brain tends to ask, "What's going on around my baby? Is the world safe, and how can I help them discover it?"

These patterns aren't rigid roles—mothers also care deeply about safety, and fathers feel their children's emotions, too. But on average, they reveal a beautifully complementary design. One parent tends to be attuned to the child's emotional life, ready to comfort and connect; the other keeps a watchful eye on the wider world, encouraging curiosity while protecting against danger. Together, these two perspectives weave a secure net beneath a child's first steps into life.

Clare Morell, my friend and tech policy guru, courageously addressed this, and lives it out herself, in an essay for *The Federalist*. It is worth reading a longer excerpt where she says,

> All too often, it seems that women espousing conservative politics make choices that fit feminists' destructive vision of life. To be clear, I am talking about women who have the practical ability to focus on rearing children but instead *choose* to prioritize their careers or other ideas of "self-actualization."...
>
> Let me be even blunter: mothers, we should not choose to delegate our main responsibility of caring for, training up, and disciplining—in a word, *parenting* our children to others for most of their waking hours. . . .
>
> This is not something we can outsource to others. . . . Mothers need to teach children to respect and love just authority, and the best way to do that is to provide it to them. We are the ones who need to invest our time in training and forming their consciences and characters. The little years lay the foundation for the rest of their lives. This is time you can't get back. And no one else will discipline or teach your children in the way you would or with the same consistency.[27]

All this research aligns perfectly with the Bible's vision for motherhood. Eve's first calling was to her husband and to the children they would bear together, and her work flowed outward from that primary vocation. When we prioritize productivity, income, or self-fulfillment over our children's needs, we displace God's design and harm those most dependent on us.

This does not mean that mothers who must work outside the home are failing their children, nor does it mean that every hour of every day must be spent side by side. Life is complex, and God's grace meets us in our limitations. But it does mean that as Christian women, we must be honest about what our children truly need and order our lives accordingly. The first three years are a sacred window of formation, one that shapes a child's emotional stability, mental health, and spiritual readiness for the rest of life. Our presence is not an accessory to their development; it is the soil in which they grow.

Heather's experience puts skin on these realities. She welcomed her first son at twenty-six and returned to her full-time job at a CPA firm six weeks later. "Going back to work was absolute misery," she told me. Her employers were kind and flexible, even allowing her to work some days from home, but she found herself watching her mom bond with her baby during the day while she worked. "It got to a point where I was jealous of the time my mom got to spend with him. When I finally turned in my notice, it was like the weight of the world lifted off my shoulders."

Needing to contribute financially, she pivoted to a home-based cake business that grew from her creative gifts. "I've always had a creative side. I made my boys' birthday cakes, and then people started saying, 'Oh, you did such a good job, could you make my child's cake?' And then a wedding cake, and then it just grew from there." She had no formal training. "We just figured it out as we went," she says of herself and her husband, Trever. "It wasn't in me to cancel an order or let someone down. They aren't going to cancel the birthday party or the wedding, so I need to figure it out and deliver."

Financially, the work helped, and it felt good to contribute. "The cake business gave me autonomy apart from being a mom. There was a lot of gratification from the cakes that were delivered. It served its purpose." But the family felt the strain. "My kids did suffer because of it. I was physically present all the time, but I was not always emotionally or mentally present. With a cake and a deadline, there were times when I couldn't physically remove my hands." Field trips slipped by as other moms stepped in. Late nights working stole sleep. What looked like an ideal compromise on paper did not always protect the attachment and availability her boys needed most. "The stress level of the cake business was affecting my husband as much as it was me. He works a lot of weekends, and when he did have a weekend off, we were doing cake deliveries. We got tired of no time together." As Trever advanced in his career and the family became debt free, they chose to shut the business down.

Heather looks back with gratitude and clarity. She does not regret working when it was needed, but she would choose differently now. "If I had to do it over again, I would have chosen something like bookkeeping from home. The cake-making served its purpose for that season, but it stole a lot of time from the boys." Her counsel to mothers who need to work is simple and wise. Choose work that offers flexibility, is easy to pause or step away from as needed, and that does not pull your attention away when little hands need you most.

Along these lines, in her book *Being There: Why Prioritizing Motherhood in the First Three Years Matters*, Erica Komisar dives into the importance of being emotionally and physically present the first three years of a child's life.[28] Nonetheless, she recognizes that there are many cases when mothers need to work or choose to work. In those moments, she recommends being present for the major transitions in a child's day, a pattern I have worked hard to replicate: wake up, drop off/pick up, and bedtime. That way, the child can bond with their mother at those key moments, even if they are separated in between.

When we approach motherhood with this perspective, our decisions about work, schedules, and ambitions begin to look different. We stop asking, "How can I fit my children into my life?" and instead ask, "How can I build my life around their flourishing?" With this in mind, we turn now to the practical question that flows from this calling: if our children's well-being must come first, how should that shape the way we approach our work? What does faithful, wise labor look like for mothers seeking to honor God, care for their families, and live out their callings in every season?

Motherhood as Warfare

Practically speaking, what began to make motherhood feel less overwhelming to me was looking at how other mothers structured their work—ebbing and flowing in their commitments based on the needs of their children. What struck me was not that they "had it all," but that they structured their work around their children, not the other way around. Many of them had built careers in medicine, research, writing, journalism, policy, or creative work. They poured themselves into full-time work before children, but when children came, they stepped back. Some worked part-time—ten to twenty hours a week—or paused entirely for several years. Some returned to work when their children were in school; others waited much longer because of homeschooling or having larger families. Some never went back to work formally and instead embraced their home economy, supporting their husband's career, or investing further in each generation of their growing family. In every case, these women maintained flexibility. Their lives embodied Nassim Taleb's concept of "antifragility": they retained autonomy over their schedules, were not dependent on their income, and could pursue opportunities with boldness because their children's well-being came first.[29] Often, their later work was shaped by the very issues they encountered in raising their families.

The rise of remote work and creative industries after the COVID-19 pandemic has only widened these possibilities. There are more ways than ever for women to scale their work around the seasons of motherhood. Yet Scripture gives us the framework: the husband is called to be the primary provider and protector, and the wife is called to be the primary caregiver and cultivator of the home. This does not mean women must never earn an income or engage in meaningful work outside the home. Proverbs 31 paints the picture of a resourceful, enterprising wife. But it does mean that our priorities must be ordered rightly. To neglect the home to pursue work is to invert God's design.

Tiffany Justice is one among many examples of how motherhood sharpens a woman's vision and expands her leadership. Rather than limiting her influence, motherhood gave her credibility, urgency, and direction. It clarified what mattered most and propelled her into a calling far bigger than she could have imagined.

Tiffany married young and welcomed their first child at twenty-five. Together, they built a life grounded in family and shared mission. In those early years, Tiffany worked alongside her husband by assisting in his commercial construction business and devoted herself to raising their four children.

When her oldest daughter entered elementary school, Tiffany poured herself into their education. She volunteered regularly and got deeply involved in the life of the school. It was there that she noticed bigger problems—namely, unfit buildings and walkways that frequently flooded, leaving students with wet feet. Frustrated that no one in the district was stepping up, she rallied other parents and pushed for the renovations herself. This experience opened her eyes to a larger reality: many people in leadership were content to use their positions as stepping stones to higher office, while real problems affecting children and families went unaddressed.

When community members urged her to run for the school board, she agreed—and won 60 percent of the vote. Motherhood had taught her patience and humility, but it had also taught her how to lead. She often said that raising sons, in particular, gave her insight into how to work well with men. Being a wife and mother had strengthened her relational instincts, sharpened her judgment, and prepared her to engage public life with conviction. "When you become a mother," she shared with me, "everything becomes more clear."

The defining moment came during the COVID-19 pandemic. Tiffany watched as school districts surrendered their authority to health departments, bureaucracies, and federal agencies like the Centers for Disease Control and Prevention (CDC). Parents were dismissed, silenced, and treated as if their voices didn't matter. Tiffany knew something had to change.

Out of that frustration, Moms for Liberty was born. What started as a grassroots effort to empower parents grew into one of the most influential parental rights organizations in the country. Today, she serves as the Executive Vice President of Heritage Action for America, where her leadership on parental rights and education policy shapes national conversations. Her journey—from stay-at-home mom to school board member to national leader—was not a departure from motherhood but the fruit of it. Every step along the way was shaped by the priorities, skills, and convictions that motherhood formed in her. As Tiffany put it, "I don't know why feminists are so anti-child. Motherhood is the most powerful force in the world."

Motherhood is one of the primary ways women grow in maturity and leadership. It is not simply a season to endure or a stepping stone to other things. It carries deep spiritual significance and is one of the chief ways women fulfill God's creation mandate. Children are not preparation for "real life." They *are* real life. They are inherent goods, gifts to be received with joy, and arrows to be shaped with purpose. And as mothers steward them faithfully, they do not lose their influence; they expand it. Children are one of the most compelling testimonies a mother can offer the world: living, breathing evidence of her love, her priorities, and her trust in God.

Motherhood, then, is not weakness. It is *warfare*. It is not a retreat from public influence. It is the formation of souls who will go further than we can. In raising children, mothers engage in a long-term spiritual strategy, cultivating resilience, courage, and faith in a generation that will outlive them—not through swords or guns, but through the formation of the next generation.

Infertility and Pain

Childlessness by choice stands in stark contrast to the Bible's teaching on children. Choosing to reject motherhood when God has given the ability and opportunity to bear children runs against the grain of the Bible's vision for womanhood and fruitfulness. From Genesis onward, God's command to "be fruitful and multiply" is not presented as a lifestyle suggestion but as part of His created order and calling. Children are described as blessings, rewards, and arrows in the hands of a warrior. To willfully close ourselves off from that gift is to resist one of the primary ways God intends to work through us. The Christian posture is not to reject life, but to receive children as gifts when God gives them and to pursue wisdom and faithfulness when that gift seems delayed.

On the other end of this spectrum is the painful experience of infertility. For some of you reading this chapter, that call may feel like salt in a wound. You may be thinking, *Yes, I want children*, yet find yourself struggling to have them.

First, know that your longing is seen, your pain is real, and God is near to the brokenhearted. Second, this is where much of my own professional work has focused, because the number of couples facing infertility continues to rise.

And as Psalm 128 reminds us, the fear of the Lord is the beginning of wisdom. That wisdom calls us to seek understanding, to pursue restorative options, and to remember that God is neither anti-science nor anti-innovation. Children were His very good idea from the very beginning, and He often uses human skill and discovery as part of His provision.

Infertility and reproductive health conditions such as endometriosis, polycystic ovary syndrome (PCOS), progesterone deficiency, thyroid disease, insulin resistance, and male-factor infertility now affect millions of couples in the United States. Roughly 16 percent of couples face infertility, and about 13.4 percent of women—nearly 10 million—between ages 15 and 49 experience impaired fertility.[30] These are not small numbers, and they point to a broader reality: infertility is not always a singular "problem" that can be solved by a one-size-fits-all solution. Infertility is not even a standalone disease; it is a symptom of deeper health issues in the man or woman's body.[31]

Unfortunately, the standard approach to infertility care often skips over this reality. Many couples are pushed quickly toward expensive and invasive procedures like in vitro fertilization (IVF). IVF can result in a live birth for some families, but it is far from a guaranteed solution. On average, it costs $15,000–$30,000 per cycle but only leads to a live birth only about 25–30 percent of the time.[32] Success rates drop sharply with age, dipping below 10 percent for women over forty.[33] IVF also carries higher risks for both mothers and babies, including multiple pregnancies, preterm birth, low birth weight, gestational diabetes, and increased maternal complications.[34] Infants conceived via IVF face higher rates of birth defects, chromosomal anomalies, and developmental disorders.[35] All of this raises serious ethical questions about informed consent and the best standard of care. Most importantly, in the pursuit of a child, IVF ranks, selects, and destroys millions of human embryos each year. At the moment of fertilization, a human embryo is genetically complete and distinct, and so how we treat him or her matters just as much as how we treat unborn babies in the womb, children, adults with disabilities, or the elderly.

The alternative is not resignation. It is to pursue true root cause treatments and care with restorative reproductive medicine (RRM). Rather than bypassing the reproductive system, RRM works with it by diagnosing and treating the root causes of infertility and restoring the body's natural ability to conceive. This approach often addresses conditions like endometriosis or blocked fallopian tubes through targeted surgical interventions, regulating hormonal imbalances, improving metabolic health, and correcting male-factor issues. It is not a "quick fix," but it produces healthier outcomes. Over twelve to twenty-four months, RRM achieves successful pregnancies in 30–50 percent of couples—results comparable to or better than IVF's per-cycle outcomes—at a fraction of the cost and with significantly lower medical risk.[36]

The key insight here is that infertility is rarely caused by a single factor. Research shows that most couples facing infertility have four or more contributing conditions, and in up to 30 percent of cases, traditional reproductive technology doctors label the cause "unexplained," simply because conventional approaches do not dig deep enough.[37] Restorative medicine addresses this gap by treating infertility not as a disease in itself but as a symptom of underlying dysfunction that, when corrected, can restore health and fertility alike. For those wrestling with infertility, I strongly recommend finding a certified restorative reproductive medicine doctor, including a Natural Procreation Technology clinic, Fertility Education and Medical Management (FEMM), or a ChartNEO instructor.

If you are walking this road, take heart: God has not left you without help. He has given you the gift of medicine and the wisdom to steward it well. He has given you a church that prays with and for you. And most importantly, He has given you Himself.

The Tent Peg Strategy: Family Life Planning

We often encourage young women to plan for college, choose a career path, and think carefully about their finances. But rarely do we invite them to plan for marriage and motherhood with the same level of intentionality. That absence has consequences. It leaves many women unprepared for the season of life that will shape them most deeply and bear the most fruit for God's kingdom. It also feeds the false idea that marriage and children are things that "just happen" someday, instead of central callings that deserve foresight, prayer, and wisdom.

We need to change how we talk about the future. Let's make marriage and children a practical and good part of our conversations about goals, calling, and vocation, starting as young as those conversations begin. This doesn't have to be heavy-handed. It can be as simple as asking questions: "Have you thought about marriage? Have you thought about motherhood? What are your hopes, fears, or questions? What is holding you back from embracing either?" Honest, thoughtful conversations like these can help uncover deeper worries and false assumptions.

Often, hesitation toward marriage or motherhood is rooted in fear. A young woman may have seen her parents' marriage fail or witnessed infidelity tear a family apart. She may have grown up hearing women complain about motherhood, blaming their children for lost careers or dreams. She may fear losing her independence or not know how family fits into the ambitions she's been told to chase. These fears are real, and they shouldn't remain unexamined. Facing them honestly and applying the truth of God's Word to them is one of the most important steps in preparing for a faithful future.

Evie Solheim knows this firsthand. She and her husband began their family in their early twenties—well before most of their peers—because they believed deeply that "life is too short to put off what we know to be good or right." They didn't want family to be something that happened "someday," but rather a calling they pursued intentionally. "I chose to have children in my twenties in part because of a philosophy that animates a lot of my decisions," Evie explained. "Only God knows how many days we have left on this earth. That's not to say I felt like I needed to rush into anything, but I didn't want to put marriage or family on an arbitrary timeline."

Their decision meant embracing reality over cultural narratives. Many of Evie's peers believed that having children young meant sacrificing freedom or success. "There was a tweet getting dunked on recently that said something like, 'Having kids before you're 30 is how you stay generationally poor,'" she recalled. "Sure, you're not going to accumulate as much wealth in your twenties if you have children compared to if you didn't. But there are so many reasons why becoming a parent in your twenties does set you up for success later in life." As Evie put it, waiting for the "perfect time" is often just another way of avoiding adulthood: "If I decided to wait to have kids, I would just endlessly be waiting for some specific marker—like buying a house or making a certain amount of money. And I felt like there weren't really good reasons to wait."

Once fears are brought into the light, we can begin to plan intentionally. There are many ways to integrate motherhood into a meaningful, purposeful life. Some women pursue degrees or training in fields that allow for flexible work in the future, such as medicine, writing, or teaching. Others choose to work part-time during their children's early years, maintaining a license or professional foothold so they can scale their work up later. Some, like my own and Jack's mothers, step away from formal employment altogether to homeschool, volunteer, and support their families in ways that bear immense fruit for generations. Every woman's story will look different, but the common thread should be a life that prioritizes children and family first.

Evie's story illustrates this balance well. Today, she writes a column for a political magazine. She does so during nap times or in the evenings, often with the help of her parents who live nearby. That support network—along with the decision to build work around family rather than the other way around—has allowed her to pursue meaningful work without sacrificing her presence in her children's lives. "You just need to be able to have honest conversations with your spouse about what your non-negotiables are and do your best to achieve them," she says. For her, that means keeping family life central and fitting professional work around it.

1. Examine Your Heart Before the Lord

A practical step in this process is to take an honest inventory of your thoughts and feelings about motherhood. Begin this process in God's Word and before the Lord in prayer. Ask God to reveal your thoughts and feelings about marriage and motherhood. Be honest and write down what comes to mind. Most importantly, write down Bible verses that relate, too.

2. Identify Your Fears or Hesitations

What concerns arise when you think about family life? What fears surface? Are you worried about pregnancy and childbirth? About finances, your health, or finding a godly husband? Are you afraid of losing freedom or not fulfilling your potential? Bring each fear into the light, remembering that "God gave us a spirit not of fear but of power and love and self-control" (2 Timothy 1:7). It is worth considering how your own childhood and family of origin is shaping your thoughts about your own marriage and motherhood.

3. Bring Your Concerns to God in Prayer

Lay every concern before Him. Ask God to shape your desires according to His will and to give you peace that surpasses understanding as you learn to trust in God's good plan for marriage and motherhood (Philippians 4:6–7).

4. Seek Wisdom from Faithful Women

Find mature, godly women who have walked through marriage and motherhood with faithfulness, joy, and God's Word on her lips. Listen to her stories, ask honest questions, and learn from her example.

5. Intentionally Plan for Your Future Family

Begin to think practically about how you can prepare for a family-centered life. Consider your education, work, finances, and community in light of God's design for marriage and family. Commit your plans to the Lord, knowing that "in all your ways acknowledge Him, and He will make straight your paths" (Proverbs 3:6). When we plan for motherhood with the same seriousness we give to careers or finances, we honor God's design and prepare ourselves to embrace one of the greatest callings He has entrusted to us. Far from limiting a woman's future, a family-oriented vision opens it wide. It roots her in purpose, draws her into deeper faith, and sets the stage for a life that is fruitful and full.

When everything around you tempts you to choose work over children, I urge you to resist and do the opposite. In many ways, it is easier to work outside the home. There are job descriptions, performance reviews, and promotions that clearly measure progress and reward effort. Motherhood, by contrast, though far sweeter and more meaningful, can often feel abstract or hard to measure on daily basis.

It takes far more effort to build the kind of intentional community that fills the void left by careerism and the loss of neighborhood and church life. It requires perseverance and creativity to build a home economy that weaves together meaningful work, wise stewardship of the household, the discipleship and teaching of children (whether homeschooled or not), and the creation of a home that exudes joy, adventure, and belonging.

This is not a choice between "real work" and "just staying home with the kids." It is a choice between work that pulls you away from the heart of family life and work that strengthens and flows from it. Some women may be paid for their work outside the home. Others may find purpose and productivity within the home, or through shared work alongside their husbands. What matters most is that your labor, whether paid or not, flows from what is good for your family and the call of Christ—not in competition with them.

We have lost the life-script that once gave women a sense of purpose and accomplishment within the home, and we need to recover it. Social media can be used to celebrate this calling, but more importantly, we must learn again from the wise women of the past.

For some, that might mean cultivating a small homestead with animals, gardens, and canned goods, like many of my aunts and uncles now do. For others, it might take the shape of creative work, hospitality, mentoring, or shared projects with their husbands. The form may differ, but the goal is the same: to reserve the best fruits of your energy for your family and home, pouring your unique gifts and interests into a life-giving, Christ-centered household under the loving leadership of your husband.

Conclusion

How we talk about motherhood matters. It shapes how we think, what we value, and the choices we make. For generations, the desire to have children was something both taught and caught. It was passed from mothers to daughters, reinforced by a culture that celebrated family and saw children as blessings. That transmission has weakened. Infertility remains a painful barrier, and singleness can delay or prevent motherhood. But one of the most overlooked reasons for declining birthrates is how women talk about motherhood itself.

Young women look to their mothers, mentors, and role models as they imagine their own futures. The tone we set, the stories we tell, and even the complaints we voice all shape their expectations.

It is time to reframe motherhood for what it truly is: providential, pleasurable, and profoundly life-giving. This is not to deny that it is difficult or sacrificial. Motherhood demands more of us than we knew we could give. Yet it also offers more than we knew we could receive. Children draw out a kind of love, patience, and creativity that nothing else can. As Jordan Peterson observed, "Your kids want to have the best relationship with you that they possibly could have. They're 100 percent on board with that idea, way more than anyone you've ever met in your life. And that means you could have the best relationship with your children than you've ever had with anyone. That's what they offer you."[38]

This truth should fill us with awe. The natural limits and sacrifices of motherhood do not diminish a woman's life; they enlarge it. They open a world of wonder, laughter, imagination, and unconditional love.

What the next generation believes about motherhood depends, in large part, on what they see and hear from us. Our daughters, sisters, and friends are watching. Our sons are, too. They are forming their expectations about family by the examples we set. If we speak with gratitude, delight, and reverence about the work of raising children, they will catch that vision. If we speak with resentment or regret, they will catch that, too.

PRINCIPLE SEVEN

Wise Counsel and Negotiation

A woman is nae a woman till time does line her face.
For 'tis time that gives her beauty, charm, and quiet grace.

—Herbert Upton, *Murder, She Wrote*

Do you see someone skilled in their work? They will serve before kings.

—Proverbs 22:29, NIV

While you would never know it by her energy or grace, Mrs. Mary Miller is well into her sixties. As the congresswoman representing Illinois' fifteenth district, she speaks with the same conviction that once guided her as a young mother on a small family farm. Her story begins in the hidden farmlands of Illinois, surrounded by cornfields, cattle, and children. To this day, she and her husband, Chris, still worship at their local Bible church and host Sunday dinners for their seven children and twenty-three (and counting!) grandchildren.

Mary married at twenty and became a mother at twenty-three, but it was in that hospital room with her first child that she began to see life differently. "I actually apologized to my mom," she told me, "because I hadn't realized how deeply she loved me until I held my own baby." As the world around her blurred right and wrong, she decided she wanted a firm foundation for her family and gave her life to Christ at twenty-four. She had never read the Bible before, and those early years were filled with discovery.

She worked alongside her husband on their farm, homeschooling their children, and building a home rooted in the Bible and service. "I gave up a lot of things others had, but I believed in seasons of life." For Mary, those years were full of meaning. "My husband and I were unified in our vision to have a big family—just to love each child and see the potential in their life. Our children are living messages to go to a time and place we may never see." When she reflects on those years, her message to younger women is steady and clear: "Be confident in your decision to make marriage and motherhood a priority. People either get excited with you if you're joyful and confident, or if they're not, at least they'll stop trying to push you around."

Her dedication to her home inspired me as she described working alongside her children and creating a home filled with purpose, music, and faith. Each of her children learned two instruments and taught younger students in the community while Mary mentored their mothers. "If you want to home educate, then you actually have to be at home," she told me, a gentle reminder that presence is the foundation of fruitful parenting. Hospitality, too, was woven into their daily life. "My kids would often ask, 'Who's coming to dinner tonight?'" she laughed, remembering how neighbors, missionaries, and friends from church were regular guests around their table. Though she loves her life now, she told me she would go back to those earlier years in a heartbeat. She encouraged me to be fully present and to treasure each moment with our young children.

When her youngest child neared graduation, Mary began to pray for direction. "I remember one evening after wrapping up a homeschool co-op and asking the Lord, 'What do You want me to do once my youngest graduates?' I even gave Him a list of ideas—as if He needed my help!" she laughs. "I prayed, 'Wherever You lead me, I want to be willing to go.'"

She never imagined that prayer would lead her to Congress. When her district's seat unexpectedly opened, few were willing to run because redistricting was expected to eliminate it within two years. But as friends and community leaders began to encourage her, they also assured her that the campaign was already fully funded. "I wouldn't have done it without my husband's full support," she said. "We prayed about it together, and I talked with our children. They were all on board, too." As her husband, an Illinois state representative, quipped in a floor speech: "Neither of us would have guessed that in our senior years we are both serving in the legislature here in Illinois and Mary in Washington, DC. Most people our age dress alike and play golf. But not us."[1]

When she was elected to Congress in 2020, Mary stepped into this new season just as she had every other with faith and determination. As Chairwoman of the Congressional Family Caucus, she now champions life from conception, defends parental rights, and pushes back against ideologies that blur the God-given differences between men and women. On the Agriculture Committee, she speaks up for farmers who feel forgotten, working to protect fertile soil, preserve family businesses, and keep American farmland in American hands. And on the Education and Workforce Committee, she stands for truth in classrooms, insisting that parents—not bureaucrats—know what's best for their children.

Through every season—wife, mother, teacher, farmer, and legislator—Mary has remained faithful to God's call. From a family farm in Illinois to the halls of Congress, her story calls women everywhere to live faithfully in their own seasons, to love their families, to speak truth with grace, and to trust that the God who calls will also equip. God's

Word flows seamlessly from her lips, and on a personal note, I found myself so encouraged and inspired when talking to her. If this is the fruit of a godly, faithful, and self-sacrificial life, then I couldn't be more on board. Like Deborah, she is one of those rare women who faithfully honored each season of her life and is now blessed with a greater realm of influence than ever before. What I love about her story, too, is that it is a living testimony that wisdom begins at home, that there is no greater joy than obedience to God's Word, and that a life yielded to God can shape a nation.

The Maiden Wars

Mary Miller's life stands in striking contrast to the life-script offered by the modern girl-boss ideal. She beautifully illustrates the seventh principle of women as wise counselors and negotiators. Indeed, as spiritual matriarchs, such women guide families, churches, communities, and nations with godly counsel and wisdom. While these stages of maturity are not restricted to age groups, marriage, or children, it takes time and spiritual refinement to experience the wise formation of a matriarch and have the hard-earned wisdom necessary to counsel others. As James B. Jordan describes it, "Becoming [matriarchs] is a third phase of our lives . . . when we have not only acquired wisdom, but have tested our wisdom through years of being [mothers] and now have acquired the ability to pass on both law and wisdom to . . . those coming after us."[2]

As maidens, we learn discernment, shrewdness, resourcefulness, and hospitality. As mothers—whether literally or spiritually—we learn to rule, to rightly judge, and to apply God's laws within the sphere He has given us. The matriarch, then, is the mature Christian woman who prays in alignment with God's will because she knows His Word and has spent her life seeking His wisdom. Her influence naturally expands beyond the household into the broader community, where she counsels, guides, and blesses the next generation.

Mary Miller's life exemplifies this. She didn't chase influence, ambition, or a career for its own sake. Instead, she was fully present and faithful in each season working beside her husband, teaching her children, and honoring God above all else.

Her life stands in stark contrast to our culture today. Our society idolizes the maiden—young, independent, and seemingly free from the responsibilities of marriage, children, and home.

This cultural script tells women that children are a burden, marriage is a means of personal fulfillment, and career is the highest calling. In doing so, it glorifies the maiden while scorning the natural and honorable progression toward mother and matriarch.

The results are easy to see. Many so-called girl-bosses hold prestigious positions in politics and business but often at the cost of faithfulness to marriage and motherhood as they prioritize getting ahead, showing that they can hold their own with male colleagues whose own wives manage their household for them, or an unwillingness to step away from the feeling of inclusion that work brings. In our pursuit of eternal youth and self-empowerment, we have traded the deep wisdom that comes only through a disciplined, faithful life.

Just as women reach a crucial turning point in their life, established and growing in the wisdom of a "mother," so many see the looming years of motherhood as a loss of all that they hold dear, rather than the sweet and potent refinement of it. Remember, only Lady Wisdom offers wine. Lady Folly, who rejects the wisdom of the matriarch, only offers sweet water and stolen bread. Addicting, perhaps, like soda, but lacking in the restorative and transformative properties present in fermented wine.

These women go all in on the *Eat, Pray, Love* mantra of self-love, youthfulness at all costs, divorce if your husband holds you back, sexual experimentation, and perhaps children—as long as they don't take up too much of your time. They try to keep it hot but only end up burning down the house they have been given. As Elisabeth Elliot, missionary and author, goes on to say in her book *Let Me Be a Woman*, "The woman who defines her liberation as doing what she wants, or not doing what she doesn't want is, in the first place, evading responsibility. Evasion of responsibility is the mark of immaturity. The Women's Liberation Movement is characterized, it appears, by this very immaturity. While telling themselves that they've come a long way, that they are actually coming of age, they have retreated to a partial humanity. . . . By refusing to fulfill the whole vocation of womanhood, she settles for a caricature, a pseudo-personhood."[3] Elisabeth Elliot, a true matriarch of the faith herself, does not pull any punches. What we call progress, she flatly rejects as little more than an immature and dehumanizing worldview that keeps women enslaved to their passions of me, myself, and I.

In many ways, today's "Maiden Wars" are a modern revival of the "Mommy Wars" that dominated conversations from the 1990s through the early 2010s. Those debates—stay-at-home versus working moms—ended not with resolution but exhaustion, as captured by *The Atlantic's* 2012 article "Why Women Still Can't Have It All," which voiced the fatigue and disillusionment of an entire generation.[4]

The Mommy Wars didn't end with a revolution or resolution. They ended with fatigue. After years of judgment, comparison, and competing ideals, many women realized how fruitless much of it was. Without a clear path forward, the conversation faded, but the pressure didn't. Women were left tired and disoriented, caught in a lose-lose cycle of work, financial needs, career ambitions, and the unpredictable needs of children. Seeing this, more and more women have begun delaying—or forgoing—marriage and children altogether. And so, we've entered a new era: the Maiden Wars. This is, in many ways, a further regression in our pursuit of maturity. It is also why the so-called conservative girlboss—*but she has kids! Unlike those leftists*—will ultimately fail.

Thankfully, the Bible tells a much different, and much better story than our culture does. Through its pages we read of women who experienced the full joy that comes through wise and faithful living—women, animated by their love for God and the peace that comes from being fully present in your season, such that their stories still inspire us today, thousands of years later.

The Wise Women of the Bible Are Speaking Now

The matriarchs of the Bible often hold the most public roles of all women, speaking to or on behalf of cities, nations, or her leaders. They are time-tested in faithfulness, serving as envoys of wisdom who offer counsel, discernment, and confirmation of God's Word.

There is a temptation to explain these women only as exceptions who act merely in the absence of godly men. Deborah, for instance, is often placed at the center of complementarian and egalitarian debates. One side argues that her leadership as a prophetess and Mother of Israel only exists because there were too few faithful men; the other uses her example to justify female pastors. Neither view fully captures the truth. Deborah *did* live in a time of weak male leadership, yet that failure did not create her wisdom; it revealed it. Like the wise matriarchs who would follow her, Deborah offered counsel to leaders, guidance to her people, and remembrance of God's faithfulness in a time of uncertainty.

It is even more mistaken to frame Deborah as a proto–female pastor, priest, or so-called shepherd. Men alone were priests in the Old Testament, though women did serve in assistant roles at the tabernacle, and possibly wrote music for its worship. Deborah, though, was never a priest in Israel, and her example does not overturn the Bible's clear teaching that pastoral authority and public teaching in the church are entrusted to qualified men (see 1 Timothy 2:12: "I do not permit a woman to teach or to exercise authority over a man; rather, she is to remain quiet"). To force her story into narrow modern categories misses the unique strength and purpose of her calling.

Deborah's position is worth noting. The Bible does not place her among the male elders at the city gate, the traditional seat of civic power, or have her teaching in the temple. Instead, like Lady Wisdom, she sat elevated under a palm tree in the hill country. From there she offered judgment and counsel to those who sought her wisdom.

Deborah led in a distinctly feminine way. She did not enter the Temple or perform priestly duties, but she spoke with prophetic conviction and steadiness. People came to her because they trusted her walk with God.

As a leader over Israel, Deborah falls into the "8 percent rule" category. Indeed, of the twelve judges listed in the book of Judges, Deborah is the only woman. This means that while there are certainly women who faithfully lead in the public square in elevated positions of power, Deborah's example shows it is more an exception to the rule than the standard we should pursue.

In that sense, Deborah's application for us today closely resembles the wise older women in the church: those who mentor younger women, offer trusted counsel to pastors and leaders, and faithfully hold the memory and culture of the community. They may not hold formal positions, but their influence is deep and enduring.

The wise women of the Bible emerge from their years of faithfulness, humility, and obedience. Their strength is tested over time, and when they speak, their words carry weight. Rather than forcing them into modern molds of leadership, we would do well to meet these women as the Bible presents them. We have much to learn from their virtues and their vision for our own lives today.

This raises several questions: Who are these wise matriarchs? How do they act when others fail? What posture do they take when leadership falters?

Women tend to act in three ways, especially under pressure, revealing their true character:

The Do Nothings: Some women in the Bible respond to conflict, loss, or failure by doing nothing at all. They freeze, look back, or enable sin or foolish behavior. They may mean well, but their passivity or willful disobedience allows sin and sorrow to take root.

The Replacers: Others may seek to replace the men who have failed by assuming full authority in their place. It does not restore or rebuild proper hierarchies but establishes a matriarchy or anarchy.

The Restorers: The women Scripture commends, however, most often work within the existing family or social structure to fulfill their God-given role. They speak truth when it is needed, offer wise judgment when others hesitate, confirm God's Word, and preserve life through humble, courageous action. They neither abandon the house nor take it over; they (re)build it with wisdom.

The Do Nothings

Some women in the Bible remind us that doing nothing can be just as destructive as doing wrong, especially when fear, bitterness, or greed keep us from moving forward in faith. Like Lot's wife, Michal, and Sapphira, we risk losing the life God longs to give us.

Take Lot's wife in the book of Genesis. When the angels led her family out of Sodom before destroying the city, they warned, "Escape for your life. Do not look back or stop anywhere in the valley. Escape to the hills, lest you be swept away" (Genesis 19:17). "But Lot's wife, behind him, looked back, and she became a pillar of salt" (Genesis 19:26). Her backward glance was more than curiosity; it revealed divided loyalty. Her heart lingered in the city God was judging. In the same way, when we cling to what God is calling us to leave behind, we lose our ability to move forward.

Michal, the daughter of Saul and wife of David, offers another warning. Early in their story, she saved David's life, but years later she despised him when he danced before the Lord in worship. The Bible records, "As the ark of the Lord came into the city of David, Michal the daughter of Saul looked out of the window and saw King David leaping and dancing before the Lord, and she despised him in her heart" (2 Samuel 6:16). Her bitterness isolated her from the joy of God's presence. Rather than joining the celebration, she stood apart in judgment, and "Michal the daughter of Saul had no child to the day of her death" (2 Samuel 6:23). She allowed bitterness to take root in her heart, and she was never able to move past the hurt she felt.

Sapphira, following her husband Ananias, chose sinful complicity. When he decided to lie about a financial offering, she agreed to the deception. "And Peter said to her, 'Tell me whether you sold the land for so much.' And she said, 'Yes, for so much.' But Peter said to her, 'How is it that you have agreed together to test the Spirit of the Lord? Behold, the feet of those who have buried your husband are at the door, and they will carry you out'" (Acts 5:8–9). Her lie was not in godly submission to her husband, nor does the Bible parrot the modern lie that women had no agency (if anything, the stories we have explored in this book should make it very clear women have had and do have a high level of God-given agency), and it cost her life. Her dishonest agreement with her husband enabled both their sinful behaviors. So-called unity when it is based on a lie always ends in death—either of the person, an organization, a movement, or a church.

The "Do Nothings" show us how deadly sin, sluggishness, or nostalgically holding on to past hurts or possessions are. In these stories, there seemed to be the belief that what was ahead of them was not as good as what was behind them. So, they refused to let go, even choosing sin over courageously stepping into what the Lord had for them in a new season.

As in the case of Lot's Wife, Michal, and Saphira, they froze, looked back, or actively sinned due to their own envy, greed, or bitterness—all sins the Bible calls us to repent and get rid of. Faith does not look back like Lot's wife, stand contemptuously aloof like Michal, or deceive like Sapphira. It trusts that active obedience to God, even when it means the death of things we hold dear, is the only life-giving path forward.

The Replacers

Some women in the Bible respond to crisis or disorder by trying to take control. Instead of trusting God to restore what is broken, they grasp for power that is not theirs to hold.

Miriam's story shows both the temptation to replace others and the grace of restoration. As a young girl, she showed remarkable courage and discernment when she watched over her baby brother Moses at the river. When Pharaoh's daughter found him, "Then his sister said to Pharaoh's daughter, 'Shall I go and call you a nurse from the Hebrew women to nurse the child for you?'" (Exodus 2:7). Her wisdom saved Moses's life and preserved God's promise. Later, when Israel crossed the Red Sea, she led the women in worship: "And Miriam sang to them: 'Sing to the Lord, for he has triumphed gloriously; the horse and his rider he has thrown into the sea'" (Exodus 15:21).

The Bible describes Miriam as a prophetess; her leadership was forged throughout her time in Egypt and the many years wandering in the desert. Yet in Numbers 12, her discernment faltered: "Miriam and Aaron spoke against Moses because of the Cushite woman whom he had married, for he had married a Cushite woman. And they said, 'Has the Lord indeed spoken only through Moses? Has he not spoken through us also?' And the Lord heard it" (Numbers 12:1–2). What began as complaint about Moses's wife revealed deeper pride and rivalry. The Lord Himself defended Moses, saying, "Hear my words: If there is a prophet among you, I the Lord make myself known to him in a vision; I speak with him in a dream. Not so with my servant Moses. He is faithful in all my house" (Numbers 12:6–7). Miriam, followed by Aaron, made herself equal with Moses, attempting to contradict his leadership. In response to this, God struck Miriam with leprosy. Still, Moses pleaded, "O God, please heal her—please" (Numbers 12:13), and after seven days outside the camp, she was restored (Numbers 12:15). Miriam's pride brought discipline, yet mercy followed. She tried to replace Moses and his unique relationship with God with her own insight, and God swiftly showed her the folly of her ways.

Jezebel showed the spirit of replacement at its worst. The Bible says, "And Ahab the son of Omri did evil in the sight of the Lord, more than all who were before him . . . he took for his wife Jezebel the daughter of Ethbaal king of the Sidonians, and went and served Baal and worshiped him" (1 Kings 16:30–31). Jezebel's influence pulled Ahab and Israel away from the covenant of the Lord and into open idolatry.

Her replacement began with God's priests. "Jezebel cut off the prophets of the Lord" (1 Kings 18:4) and fed hundreds of false prophets at her own table. She sought to silence the word of God and install her own religion in its place. When Elijah called for the contest on Mount Carmel, she stood behind the prophets of Baal who cried out from morning to evening, cutting themselves as was their custom. When the Lord answered Elijah with fire and the prophets of Baal were slain, Jezebel's pride rose in fury. "Then Jezebel sent a messenger to Elijah, saying, 'So may the gods do to me and more also, if I do not make your life as the life of one of them by this time tomorrow'" (1 Kings 19:2). Her desire for control turned to vengeance against God's messenger.

Next, she subverted justice. When her husband coveted Naboth's vineyard, Jezebel mocked his weakness and took action herself. "Do you now govern Israel? Arise and eat bread and be cheerful. I will give you the vineyard of Naboth the Jezreelite" (1 Kings 21:7). She wrote letters "in Ahab's name and sealed them with his seal" (1 Kings 21:8), arranging a false trial: "Set two worthless men opposite him, and let them bring a charge against him, saying, 'You have cursed God and the king.' Then take him out and stone him to death" (1 Kings 21:10). When Ahab heard that Naboth was dead, he went down to take possession of the vineyard. The Lord sent Elijah to confront him: "You have sold yourself to do what is evil in the sight of the Lord. Behold, I will bring disaster upon you" (1 Kings 21:20–21). The Bible adds, "There was none who sold himself to do what was evil in the sight of the Lord like Ahab, whom Jezebel his wife incited" (1 Kings 21:25).

Eventually, her evil actions consumed her own house. Years later, when Jehu came to execute God's judgment, he said, "What peace can there be, so long as the whorings and the sorceries of your mother Jezebel are so many?" (2 Kings 9:22). Jezebel looked down from her window, painted her eyes, and called out in defiance. Jehu ordered, "Throw her down" (2 Kings 9:33). The word of the Lord was fulfilled: "the dogs shall eat the flesh of Jezebel" (2 Kings 9:36).

Jezebel's legacy is the ruin that comes when a woman replaces true worship with idolatry, godly authority with manipulation, and justice with envy and deceit. She corrupted her husband's soul, her household, and her nation. Her story stands as the clearest picture of how the desire to replace God's order ends in destruction.

I have seen this same pattern play out many times, even within the church and Christian families. Some women, often out of genuine care or frustration, try to take control of what is not theirs to hold. Instead of using their influence to reinforce healthy order, they begin to center everything around themselves. They become intermediaries: the ones others must go through, rather than pointing people back to their rightful places of authority.

It can look spiritual or even helpful, especially when women are carrying much of the daily weight of ministry, family, or church life, but doing more does not automatically mean it is their place to lead. In God's design, our work and wisdom are meant to support and strengthen, not replace, the leadership He has established.

We see this dynamic in homes where a wife quietly overrules her husband, in churches where women become informal gatekeepers, or in friendships where advice turns into control. There's a familiar joke that when a man says, "Brothers, I've been praying about it," what he really means is that he went home and his wife disagreed. But humor aside, there is a real and valuable place for women to serve as wise advisors. The danger comes when counsel turns into control.

The Bible reminds us that women must not become busybodies or gossips. Instead, as wise counselors, women act as restorers when they help heal what is broken; they become replacers when they grasp at influence before its time. Even well-intentioned women can fall into the temptation to "manage" outcomes rather than pray, wait, and trust the Lord to lead.

Each story shows that when women subvert rightful authority, beginning with their husbands in the home, their pastors in the church, or others in leadership, disorder and strife follow. Miriam's rebellion was healed through repentance. Jezebel's ended in ruin. The difference between the two was humility before God.

The Restorers

The women the Bible commends most often take a third path. They neither abandon the house nor take it over. They work within the order God has established to preserve life, confirm His Word, and build again what sin has broken. In short, they do not replace; they restore.

Deborah

Israel had fallen again. "The people of Israel again did what was evil in the sight of the Lord after Ehud died" (Judges 4:1). God raised up Deborah who was "a prophetess, the wife of Lappidoth, [who] was judging Israel at that time" (Judges 4:4). The text identifies her as the *wife* or *woman* of Lappidoth—though the Hebrew word (*ishshah*) can mean either.

Interestingly, no man named Lappidoth appears elsewhere in Scripture. However, the word *lappidoth* itself often appears in Judges as a reference to flames or torches. It's possible that Deborah was married to a man by that name, but the phrasing may intentionally carry a double meaning. Translated differently, Deborah becomes the "woman of flames" or a fiery woman. She sat under her palm between Ramah and Bethel, offering counsel and judgment to those who came to her. She listened for God's voice and spoke what He revealed.

Seeing that the military leader Barak was not obediently leading Israel's army into battle, Deborah summoned him, asking, "Has not the Lord, the God of Israel, commanded you?" (Judges 4:6). When he replied, "If you will go with me, I will go," she agreed, but told him, "The road on which you are going will not lead to your glory, for the Lord will sell Sisera into the hand of a woman" (Judges 4:8–9). At Barak's request, Deborah agreed to accompany him to the battle. Yet, she did not go as a warrior or fight herself. She went as a wise woman and counselor. Further reinforcing Barak's weakness as a military leader, Deborah had to encourage him each step of the way. On the day of battle she said, "Up! For this is the day in which the Lord has given Sisera into your hand. Does not the Lord go out before you?" (Judges 4:14).

After Israel's victory, Deborah sang a song of praise with Barak. She blessed Jael as "most blessed of women" (Judges 5:24) and called herself "a mother in Israel" (Judges 5:7). Like Miriam after the parting of the Red Sea, Deborah's song sealed Israel's victory with worship. She did not try to replace Barak, despite his delayed and cowardly disobedience, nor did she try to install herself as a ruler. Her wise counsel and guidance spurred the people on in their faithful obedience to God.

The Wise Woman of Abel Beth-Maacah

Another restorer appears in 2 Samuel 20. When the rebel Sheba fled to the northern city of Abel Beth-Maacah and Joab came to destroy it, an unnamed "wise woman" intervened. From the city wall she called out, "They used to say in former times, 'Let them but ask counsel at Abel,' and so they settled a matter. I am one of those who are peaceable and faithful in Israel. You seek to destroy a city that is a mother in Israel. Why will you swallow up the heritage of the Lord?" (2 Samuel 20:18–19).

Her courage and discernment preserved her people. She negotiated with Joab, persuaded her city to hand over the traitor, and ended the siege. The text concludes simply: "So [Joab] blew the trumpet, and they dispersed from the city, every man to his home" (2 Samuel 20:22). Without sword or army, she saved a city through wisdom and words rightly spoken. She stood on the wall and spoke life into the chaos below.

Huldah

Generations later, when the Book of the Law was rediscovered during Josiah's reign, the king's messengers sought the prophetess Huldah for confirmation. She declared both judgment and mercy: disaster would come upon Judah for its idolatry, but because Josiah's heart was tender, "your eyes shall not see all the disaster that I will bring upon this place" (2 Kings 22:20).

Huldah's life of worship, study of God's Word, and prayer meant that when she was called upon, she could faithfully confirm, discern, and offer guidance concerning God's Word. Her wisdom restored the fear of the Lord to a generation that had forgotten His law.

Anna

Centuries later, another prophetess waited in the temple. Anna "did not depart from the temple, worshiping with fasting and prayer night and day" (Luke 2:37). When Mary and Joseph brought the infant Jesus to be presented to the Lord, Anna recognized Him as the promised Redeemer. "She began to give thanks to God and to speak of Him to all who were waiting for the redemption of Jerusalem" (Luke 2:38).

Her long faithfulness was crowned with sight. She saw Wisdom Incarnate and became one of the first heralds of the gospel. Like Huldah and Deborah, she confirmed God's Word, this time in His flesh and blood.

One of the most striking examples of this kind of faithfulness is Pietje Baltus, a woman who confronted the Dutch Reformed pastor and theologian Abraham Kuyper. He is best known for his unapologetic declaration that "There's not a square inch in the whole domain of human existence over which Christ, who is Lord over all, does not exclaim, 'Mine!'"[5] Yet before he became the titan of the faith that he is today, he held to a liberal theology that downplayed the infallibility of the Bible and the sovereignty of God.

In 1863, Kuyper began his first pastoral role in the Dutch village of Beesd. While many congregants boycotted his church because of his theology, he sought to meet with them. Then in her mid-thirties, Pietje Baltus welcomed him into her home but did not mince words: "You do not give us the true bread of life."[6] She challenged his faith with her deep Reformed beliefs, sparking a renewal in Kuyper that led him to embrace the authority of God's Word. "For the rest of his life, Kuyper kept a photo of Pietje on his desk."[7]

What I love about this story is that this woman didn't seek to replace Kuyper as the pastor because she had a better understanding of the Bible or was a more talented speaker. She met with him, reasoned with him, and through her faith and courage strengthened his calling. Her words helped restore his theology, his ministry, and his devotion to Christ. Through her obedience, the Lord renewed one man. And through that man, the faith of a nation.

The restorers lead through wise counsel and negotiation. They do not seek to replace those in authority or undermine those who God has established as rulers and leaders. They do, however, frequently lead other women in praising God; sing blessings over the next generation; confirm God's Word—a practice which requires a life of careful study and a love for God's Word—when others hesitate, capitulate, or delay; and intervene on behalf of their city or nation, and do so as mothers in Israel such that they maintain their feminine and maternal touch.

The Tent Peg Strategy: Seeking the Matriarch

Now more than ever, we need two kinds of women: wise matriarchs and young women eager to learn. Many women in my generation feel the absence of older women who can speak meaningfully into their lives. In our enthusiasm for youth, culture has often deferred to the young rather than honoring the godly wisdom of older women and calling them to instruct the next generation.

Some older women may feel unqualified or out of touch with the rapid changes in culture, while others may hesitate because they were never mentored themselves. Yet neither reason is sufficient. Wisdom is timeless. Though technology and trends change, the Word of God does not. The task of an older woman is not to master every cultural shift but to faithfully apply the Bible to it. Even a woman who never had a mentor can pass on what she has learned about faithfulness, failure, and walking with God through every season.

At the same time, a troubling pattern has emerged in which some older women urge younger women to delay marriage and/or children in favor of career ambitions, implying that they wish they had, too. Not only has this advice left many in younger generations lonely, disconnected, and fearful that family will hold them back in life, but it doesn't take into account the positive benefits and flexible, home-based options that are available more now than ever.

In many situations, what women truly need is specific, personalized wisdom that speaks directly to who you are with your unique story, relationships, strengths, and struggles. Broad or overly generalized advice can only go so far. And when guidance becomes too rigid or prescriptive—such as declaring, "It's wrong for women to work outside the home"—it often becomes more of a stumbling block than a help. Pursuing wisdom requires discernment for your particular season and calling, not a one-size-fits-all formula.

The Bible gives us a clear vision of this path:

- **1 Timothy** lays the *foundation*: spiritual maturity begins with guarding doctrine, cultivating inward holiness, and understanding a woman's calling within God's order. It's about personal formation and character.
- **Titus 2** then moves to *expression*: how that inner godliness is lived out in relationships, marriage, and witness to others. It's about conduct and influence.
- **1 Peter 3** becomes the *culmination*: the mature woman's role in teaching and training the next generation. It's about multiplication and mentorship.

Put another way, these passages outline a clear progression of spiritual maturity emphasizing our formation, our faithfulness, and our fruitfulness.

Step 1: Foundation—1 Timothy

I first turned to 1 Timothy to study its teachings on godly women. The Apostle Paul, writing to his protégé Timothy, doesn't begin with behavior lists or gender roles. He begins with a warning: watch out for false teaching, shallow doctrines, and those who "devote themselves to myths and endless genealogies" that pull believers away from the heart of the gospel (1 Timothy 1:4). Later, Paul reinforces this point saying, "Have nothing to do with irreverent, silly myths. Rather train yourself for godliness" (1 Timothy 4:7).

Today, these "myths" might refer to the cultural fascination with the occult, goddess spirituality, the "divine feminine," or even the modern "you can have it all" girl-boss mindset. Patricia Patnode captured this connection vividly in an essay for *The American Mind* after attending a modern witch coven. "The similarities between the language used by the coven and among my own decidedly non-witch friends was striking," she wrote. "'Are we accidentally practicing witchcraft?' I wondered to myself."[8]

She described how common practices such as vision boards, affirmations written on mirrors, horoscope mugs, and endless advice about "soft living" or "feminine energy" mirror rituals found in Wicca or pagan spirituality. Videos titled "Elevate Your Lifestyle," "Channel Divine Femininity," and "Leverage Your Light Feminine Energy" fill TikTok and Instagram, especially as women make resolutions for the new year. Indeed, women are often told to speak our desires into existence, to align our "energy" with the universe, and to manifest abundance and love through positive thinking.

These practices may look harmless, but they are the opposite of godly wisdom and maturity. Instead of pursing godly wisdom, which begins with the fear of the Lord, these practices tell women that *they* are divine goddesses who can control their destiny through willpower and words. They promise hidden knowledge and self-mastery, repeating the same deception the serpent offered Eve in the garden. The lie is that

God is holding something back and that we can claim it for ourselves. That path does not lead to freedom. It leads to confusion and death. No wonder Paul made such a point to address it first. To grow in wisdom, we must put off such practices and train ourselves for godliness.

Paul continues, "Women should adorn themselves in respectable apparel, with modesty and self-control, not with braided hair and gold or pearls or costly attire, but with what is proper for women who profess godliness—with good works" (1 Timothy 2:9–10).

How we dress reflects what we believe and what we value. Whatever our culture or style, modesty, self-control, and good works should be at the center of a wise woman's life. Paul reminds us that godliness grows from the heart, not from appearance. True beauty comes from a character formed by the Bible, not by what we wear or own. Status is not measured by a designer label or a polished image but by the fruit of godliness shown in everyday faithfulness.

Modesty is not only about how much skin you show. It is about knowing how to dress in a way that fits the setting and honors God. A bathing suit may be fine for a day at the beach, but it would be inappropriate for the workplace. A formal gown may fit a gala but would distract in a church service. And yet, how good and glorious it is when a woman is rightly adorned at a gala, or her own wedding day, such that her dress rightly reflects, rather than distracting from, the event.

I learned this when I volunteered at my church's food pantry in high school. I wore an outfit typical for me, including stylish jewelry, colorful clothes, and a cute pair of boots. But every conversation turned into comments about my clothes. What I wore had become a distraction, even though I had not intended it to be. Amy Carmichael, a missionary to Japan and India, had a similar experience. Her first attempt to tell a woman about Christ failed because the woman became distracted by her fur gloves. Neither of us had sinned by what we wore, but both of us learned the same truth: if something we wear draws attention away from Christ or disrupts fellowship, it is not worth it.

Paul's point is clear. A godly woman exercises discernment and self-control in all areas of life, even in how she dresses. We need both the wisdom to discern what is modest in each setting and the self-control to live it out, so that our good works can continue without distraction. The question is not whether something is technically modest, but whether it helps or hinders the gospel and hospitality. There will always be people who envy or misjudge, and we are not responsible for their reactions. But wisdom means considering how our choices affect others and being willing to set aside anything that clouds the gospel or distracts from godly living.

Paul's vision of formation continues as he describes the women connected to the church's leadership. "Their wives likewise must be dignified, not slanderers, but sober-minded, faithful in all things" (1 Timothy 3:11). These traits describe a woman who can be trusted, who guards her speech, and who stands firm in her convictions.

Later, Paul offers one of the most beautiful portraits of a faithful woman in his instructions concerning widows: "Let a widow be enrolled if she is not less than sixty years of age, having been the wife of one husband, and having a reputation for good works: if she has brought up children, has shown hospitality, has washed the feet of the saints, has cared for the afflicted, and has devoted herself to every good work" (1 Timothy 5:9–10). In these instructions, Paul shows us the marks of godly formation that we should all aim for in each season of life.

Taken together, Paul points to:

- Faithfulness in marriage
- Purposeful motherhood
- Lifestyle of service and hospitality
- Wise management of the home
- Sobriety and self-control
- Devotion to good works
- Vigilance against the enemy

Paul lays the foundation, but the application happens through older women helping younger women learn how to live this out in practice.

Taken together, formation means guarding doctrine, cultivating inward holiness, and ordering one's life around good works that strengthen the family and the household of faith. Women who do so give the devil no foothold. They resist the temptation to drift into distraction or self-indulgence, keeping their eyes on the greater purpose of serving Christ.

Step 2: Expression—Titus 2

Titus 2 shows what faithfulness looks like in the wise woman's life, beginning with her most intimate relationships. Paul writes, "Older women likewise are to be reverent in behavior, not slanderers or slaves to much wine. They are to teach what is good, and so train the young women to love their husbands and children, to be self-controlled, pure, working at home, kind, and submissive to their own husbands, that the word of God may not be reviled" (Titus 2:3–5).

Paul's instructions begin with older women. He doesn't tell Titus or the male elders to disciple women personally. Instead, he entrusts this work to those women who have walked with God through the ups and downs of real life. Their job is to teach and model what faithfulness looks like in ordinary days including how to love a husband well, raise children with patience, and live with peace and self-control. Similarly, Paul is also clear in Ephesians 5:25–33 that for married couples, the husband bears the responsibility to lead and teach his own wife in godliness "that he might sanctify her, having cleansed her by the washing of water and the word" (Ephesians 5:26).

This model of mentorship is deeply personal. It cannot be replaced by podcasts, social media, or self-help advice. Real discipleship happens face to face, through friendship, accountability, and honest conversation. A younger woman needs someone who knows her story.

What are the key things older women are to teach younger women?

- To love their husbands and children
- To be self-controlled, pure, and kind
- To work at home
- To be submissive to their own husbands

When a woman gossips, speaks harshly, drinks too much, lets bitterness take root, or pushes her family to the side, she is preaching a gospel contrary to Jesus Christ. One that says that God's design isn't good, that His Word isn't enough, and that His blessings don't satisfy. But when a woman is faithful, kind, self-controlled, and joyful in her closest relationships, her life tells a different story. It shows that God is good and that His ways can be trusted.

Paul also gives the reason behind these commands: "that the word of God may not be reviled." Our actions shape how others see the gospel. When we are kind, disciplined, and faithful, our lives declare that God's design is good. When we live carelessly or selfishly, we tell the world that the Lord isn't sufficient.

Like many of you, I've done the visible good works. I've gone on mission trips, served in homeless shelters, helped with inner-city ministries, and volunteered at church. Those things matter. They're good and important. But Paul reminds us to look closer to the places where our faith is tested the most. It's in our closest relationships that spiritual maturity really shows and the gospel shines the brightest. A woman can speak beautifully, serve tirelessly, and still miss what God values most: being faithful in her home, her marriage, and her inner life.

In practice, this looks like older women intentionally mentoring younger ones, opening their homes, and sharing what they've learned. It looks like younger women taking the time to ask hard questions, hear the advice of others, and when it aligns with the Bible, be willing to apply it.

This is also why it is so important to find godly, older women you know in real life where you can see the fruit of their lives up close. And they, in turn, should know you and your life. As with all things, we should "test everything [and] hold fast [to] what is good" (1 Thessalonians 5:21).

I learned this way the hard way when I was in college. I had one mentor who I had known for many years who lived in my hometown. Let's call her Amy. Amy and I had walked through some of the hardest years of my life together. She was a gift from God bringing friendship, perspective, and many sweet memories at Waffle House each Thursday. She had been there through two relationships, so when I started dating my now-husband Jack, my questions about children and what I wanted from life played out against a backdrop of old fears and unresolved conflict. But Amy wasn't married and had chosen not to have children. From her perspective, my anxiety about the relationship seemed like a sign that it had run its course. Sadly, rather than affirming the goodness of marriage and children, she encouraged me to end it.

I have no doubt she meant well, but her advice crossed healthy boundaries and only deepened my fear. Instead of pausing to clear my head or involve other godly counselors, I let our conversation push me toward a rash decision: breaking up with Jack. (A season, of course, that God ultimately redeemed and used to teach me the goodness of marriage and children, though it was a painful lesson.)

When I realized how foolish I had been, I felt very hurt and let down by Amy, but also disappointed in my myself. I had elevated her voice, much like King Ahasuerus did with Haman, above everyone else's. I was desperate for wisdom and guidance but didn't follow biblical wisdom about how to seek it.

It reminds me of a story Abigail Shrier shared in her book *Bad Therapy: Why the Kids Aren't Growing Up*. Reflecting on her own time in therapy, she describes a close relationship with a counselor she saw during a lonely season of her life. When Abigail shared that her boyfriend had proposed, her therapist responded with caution, saying she didn't think Abigail was ready. Coming from someone she trusted, that warning carried weight. What I appreciate about Abigail's response, however, is that instead of reacting impulsively or accepting the advice without question, she reflected on it, disagreed respectfully, and decided to move on from such frequent sessions. When therapy was helpful, it served her well, but when it crossed a line, she had the self-awareness to step back.[9]

As more and more people now turn to therapy to fill the void once occupied by parents, friends, pastors, and mentors, *Bad Therapy* explores the many errors that flow from a culture increasingly outsourcing relationships, and even their own self-reflections, to an over-psychologized culture. Shrier traces the damage this has caused in American life, from the wave of false abuse stories in the 1990s to the rise of "do whatever feels good" morality and even the affirmation of the so-called transgender movement.

That is why it is more important than ever for young women to seek godly, older mentors and for older women to seek out younger women to mentor in the church. Interestingly, a 2025 study from Barna found that while Generation Z members (those born from 1997 to 2007) attend church at higher rates than older generations—a wonderful development all on its own—38 percent of Gen Z women "ages 18–24 now identify as religiously unaffiliated, a notable statistic that sits higher than their male peers."[10] Furthermore, this "no faith" group "report the lowest rates of Bible reading, prayer and church attendance among their peers."[11] For those watching recent elections or TikTok, these numbers are far from surprising. Still, the point to an important evangelistic need and opportunity in the Church today. Among the research findings, Barna "suggest[ed] that intergenerational connection may be key to restoring faith and belonging among Gen Z women."[12] One way to model faith, and overcome the loneliness many young women feel today, is to invest in intergenerational relationships and model a real, vibrant, and life-giving faith in Jesus Christ.

Of course, some young women aren't open to real mentorship, but it's also true that many older women have not positioned themselves as mentors or pursued younger women in the church. This is something Mrs. Miller emphasized to me as well.

In her thirties, she and Chris met an older couple who invested in them and modeled a life of faith. "Everybody should have a mentor," she says. "It's so important. If it's someone a stage ahead of you, that's good. Look for someone who knows the Word of God and believes it." Over time, their own home became a gathering place for others. "There were traffic jams in our driveway," Mary laughs. "So many moms came to share their struggles. It was very draining, and I remember wondering, 'Where are all the other women?'" Those years gave her a heart for community and discipleship. "We need to mix age groups," she says. "Older people come to life with the energy of youth, and young people learn so much from the wisdom of older believers." Even now, she encourages women to use their gifts for God's service. "Some women are busy with golf or the gym, and that's fine, but the goal of the Christian life is service. Ask God to show you the opportunities—maybe teaching, supporting Christian schools, or mentoring others."

Like Titus 2 outlines, it is essential to find an older mentor who is self-controlled in speech, appetite, and dress; pure and kind; who stewards her home well; respects and honors her husband; and loves her children with the self-sacrificial presence of someone like Mrs. Miller.

In response to a season where an older, godly mentor was not obvious, my friend Carmel told me, "There are too many elders who give bad advice about marriage and family. I am trying to become the matriarch I want to see in the world."

Step 3: Culmination—1 Peter 3

1 Peter explores the fruit of a well-formed and faithful life, especially as it relates to training the next generation. Peter writes,

> Likewise, wives, be subject to your own husbands, so that even if some do not obey the word, they may be won without a word by the conduct of their wives, when they see your respectful and pure conduct.
>
> Do not let your adorning be external—the braiding of hair and the putting on of gold jewelry, or the clothing you wear—but let your adorning be the hidden person of the heart with the imperishable beauty of a gentle and quiet spirit, which in God's sight is very precious.
>
> For this is how the holy women who hoped in God used to adorn themselves, by submitting to their own husbands, as Sarah obeyed Abraham, calling him lord. And you are her children, if you do good and do not fear anything that is frightening. (1 Peter 3:1–6)

It's easy for modern readers to get hung up on phrases like "wives, be subject to your own husbands" or "Sarah obeyed Abraham, calling him lord." The common feminist critique that this passage disempowers women misses how radical it actually is. What stands out is that Peter speaks directly to women. In the first-century Roman world, women were often treated as property or second-class citizens. Yet here, Peter speaks to them as moral and spiritual agents. He does not tell husbands what to force their wives to do. He speaks to the wives themselves. God knows the worth and agency of women, and He affirms it through passages like these. Their role in the family, church, and world is essential.

Peter is saying: You, as a wife, may be how your unbelieving husband is won to Christ—not by arguing, pleading, or dominating him, but through a faithful and respectful life that reflects the gospel. Thus, fruitfulness is the outward result of a faithful life. It's the influence that comes when a woman's character and conduct reflect Christ so clearly that others are drawn to Him.

Conclusion

When men fail, or when the structures that should uphold righteousness crumble, God often reveals the wisdom of the women already walking in faithfulness. These are women who wait actively on God. And when their moment comes, they are ready. This is not because they grasped for influence, but because they had cultivated wisdom in the hidden places of their life. They knew when to speak, when to act, and when to remain silent. And through them, God preserved His people.

For us today, this means we don't chase recognition or grasp at power. Instead, we learn to pursue wisdom. For those who have been failed by leaders, husbands, or communities, resist the temptation to let bitterness harden your heart. Instead, learn from the strength of the women we have studied. Let God form in you the kind of wisdom that brings peace in conflict, hope in despair, and clarity in confusion.

For those who lead—pastors, husbands, mentors, and fathers—cherish and listen to the wise women God has placed in your life. Their insight is not a threat to your calling, but often the very help you need to fulfill it well. Like David before Abigail, Barak before Deborah, or Josiah before Huldah, learn to recognize the wisdom of a woman shaped by truth and submission to God.

CONCLUSION

Wise Women, Rise Up!

There will be those who, undoubtedly, take issue with my naming this book after Jael, especially since there are so many other godly women in the Bible with a lot less textual baggage to choose from. Why name the book after someone whose actions may be interpreted as questionable at best? In short, because, as I hope I showed you, there is far more to her story than meets the eye, especially for women today. When we come across stories in the Bible that don't quite make sense, our first inclination shouldn't be to dismiss them as just more examples of sinful people we have nothing to learn from as New Testament Christians. Instead, we should pause and take the opportunity to look closer and ask: What is God trying to show us here through His Word?

What stands out to me is that while Jael was put in a position she never should have been in during Israel's war with the Canaanites, her faithfulness to her home and her resourcefulness enabled her to act when Israel's enemy came stumbling to her doorstep. Just as God prophesied in Genesis 3:15, she became one of the many "head-crushers" throughout the Bible who foreshadowed Jesus's ultimate victory over sin and death on the cross. Despite her imperfect circumstances, and the morally questionable way she went about things, I am in awe of God's mercy and faithfulness in Jael's story to redeem her broken efforts and include her in His redemptive work throughout the Bible. God did not show her story as an example of a "you go, girl" warrior princess, but as a woman who faithfully served where God placed her. And yes, God blessed her greatly, placing her in the lineage of head-crushers from Eve to Mary.

Jael's story resonates deeply with me today because there are so many similarities between her time and ours: we live in a time when each man does what is right in his own eyes (a common refrain throughout the book of Judges), godly male leadership in the church and the home has faltered or been effectively replaced, and women are, in many cases, being called upon to fill the gap or are set adrift amid the modern scripts of "girl-boss" feminism.

We do not live in an ideal time, and we won't until the Lord Jesus returns again. So, the question is, what does it mean to live as faithful and wise women, given the time, place, and season you have been placed in?

When I began writing this book about the need for wise women to rise up, one thing plagued me throughout the process: while reports show a revival among young men in the United States and the Western world, young women are not following suit. For example, "*The New York Times* reported [in 2024] that, for the first time in American history, men now outnumber women in churches. The trend is especially pronounced among twenty-somethings. [That same] year, a survey by the Public Religion Research Institute found that 39% of Gen Z women identify as religiously unaffiliated, compared with just 31% of men. Among white evangelicals, young men had begun showing significantly more religiosity than women."[1] Such results mirror Barna's 2025 report where young men between the ages of thirteen and twenty-four are more likely than their female peers to read the Bible, go to church, and pray. They're also far less likely to identify as religiously unaffiliated. Indeed, in many cases, it was women who seemed to be increasingly alienated from the church, healthy father figures, and meaningful relationships.

This stark contrast made one thing clear to me: when men embrace their God-given calling, it can change the trajectory of families, churches, and even nations, yet it won't be complete without wise women serving alongside them. Indeed, it isn't a question of if men will be leaders, but if they'll be faithful or unfaithful leaders.

That is why conservative activist Charlie Kirk's example to young men was, and is, so profound. And it is why his assassination in September 2025 shook countless people to their core.

After his death, Kirk was awarded the Presidential Medal of Freedom, the highest civic praise any person can receive. He orchestrated many of the most significant political friendships of our time: from J. D. Vance and Robert F. Kennedy Jr. to President Donald Trump, and he had engaged an entire generation of Gen Z men who were otherwise tapping out and unreachable. But perhaps the greatest thing was that, upon his death, he was not primarily known for his political efforts but for his Christian faith as a follower of Jesus Christ.

After his death and at his funeral, pastors, friends, and heads of state from Secretary of State Marco Rubio to Vice President J. D. Vance boldly preached the gospel of Jesus Christ without shame. Even the president of the United States began making public comments about salvation, heaven, and his eternal soul in the weeks and months that followed.

It is not an exaggeration to say that Charlie Kirk's life pointed people to Jesus Christ. Indeed, as Charlie shared in an interview with *Deseret News*, "This is where you have to try to point them toward ultimate purposes and toward getting back to the church, getting back to faith, getting married, having children. That is the type of conservatism that I represent, and I'm trying to paint a picture of virtue, of lifting people up, not just staying angry."[2] When asked how he wanted to be remembered in an undated clip shared on X, Charlie replied, "I want to be remembered for courage for my faith. . . . The most important thing is my faith."[3] Indeed, even in the days leading up to his assassination, Charlie posted on X that "Jesus defeated death so you can live."[4] That is the ultimate legacy that he left behind. And this happened because he was a fearless and faithful combatant in our generation's central theological fight over the question of what it means to be human.

As David Glade, rector of the Christ the King Anglican church in Alexandria, Virginia, shared in a sermon, the most contentious issue of our day is not, "Who is Jesus?" or "How can man be saved?" (Those questions were asked and answered in previous centuries.) The question of our day is anthropology: What does it mean to be human? Put simply, the Church today must preach "the good news of biblical anthropology."[5] That is the theological fight of our day.

And that is exactly what Charlie did, day in and day out. We need a nation of Charlie Kirks. Men who are godly, courageous, strong, visionary, and dedicated. Who rise as protectors and providers of sound doctrine, fight for righteousness in the public square, pursue marriage and children as faithful and gentle heads, and set a vision for a nation where their families can thrive in the fullness of God's good design. Or, as Charlie pithily put it, "Get married. Have children. Build a legacy. Pass down your values. Pursue the eternal. Seek true joy."[6]

As many people have pointed out, Charlie Kirk engaged young men in politics and religion like no one else could, and in the wake of his assassination, Erika Kirk is poised to bring along the young women. Erika faithfully supported Charlie as her husband in his work, even as he wrote weekly notes asking, "How can I better serve you as a husband?" She devoted her first priorities to being a faithful wife and mother, and in the wake of unimaginable tragedy, she now stands as a powerful example of what true, fearless, and biblical womanhood looks like.

Erika embodies a woman who is afraid of no fearful thing. She forgave her husband's assassin, continued to worship, pray, and praise God for His goodness, and is showing a generation of women the precise role model they need: the beauty of a strong, smart, kind, and wise woman.

She is not a girl boss, nor is she pursuing some egalitarian ideal of sameness. Indeed, just days after Charlie's death, she said, "Your wife is not your servant. Your wife is not your employee. Your wife is not your slave. She is your helper. You are not rivals. You are one flesh, working for the glory of God." Indeed, it is worth quoting a longer portion from Erika's speech at Charlie's memorial service in September 2025. Reflecting on her husband's legacy, and her advice to men and women across the world, she said,

> Women, I have a challenge for you, too. Be virtuous. Our strength is found in God's design for our role. We are the guardians. We are the encouragers. We are the preservers. Guard your heart. Everything you do flows from it. And if you're a mother, please recognize that is the single most important ministry you have. In our home, because Charlie traveled a lot, we tried to travel with him where we could. But I made sure that when Charlie returned from work, it was his sacred landing place away from the worries of the world. I didn't make him feel guilty for being away too long or too much. Or getting home too late. I always told him home is here for you and it'll be ready for you. And I made it into this place where he wanted to be as soon as possible when he was on the road.
>
> There was no keeping score between us. We were a team working together for the same mission. I never wanted to be the one standing between Charlie and the task that God prepared for him. I had set for him, and I knew Charlie would always do his best to help me with the same. My marriage with Charlie was the best thing that ever happened to me, and I know it was the best thing that ever happened to him as well. He wanted everyone to experience that joy.[7]

Such a vision of marriage is the salve needed to overcome the battle of the sexes. There are few messages that speak to the heart of women more deeply. Yes, it may elicit fear, and some may recoil at the words, but they strike a chord deep within each person about the power of God's good design for marriage, even if one rejects it.

My goal in writing this book was to provide a guide to seven of the biblical principles essential for today's women of faith. Rather than continuing to debate girl-boss feminism or the tradwife movement, I wanted to offer a deeply biblical vision of womanhood that our generation can build upon as faithful followers of Christ. Each principle is essential for godly women who are rooted in God's Word, faithful in prayer and worship, and devoted to good works. To raise a generation of faithful women, inspired by the example of Erika Kirk, we must begin and end with what the Bible teaches.

Now, more than ever, women need *discernment* to distinguish between good and evil, even when culture or their emotions cloud the way.

This requires woman to be *shrewd* in all things. Such shrewdness doesn't break laws or subvert authority, but it does direct women to be wise and prudent when they act, whether it is navigating tensions within one's family, fostering unity between siblings, or doing good work in your community. I think of this principle often in my work as a policy researcher covering issues such as IVF, surrogacy, biotechnology, and restorative reproductive medicine. Building coalitions, rallying people around a cause, debating publicly or privately, and framing messaging effectively are essential to whether we gain or lose ground on an issue. That requires us to act shrewdly and to understand our opponents as we fight for what is good.

Taken together, these two principles lead us to the third one: *resourcefulness* in directing when, where, and how we work. It is not about acting like men, but about using the tools, skills, and responsibilities God has given us as women to crush the head of the serpent wherever it appears. Most importantly, this is accomplished in and through the home of faithful women, beginning with their husbands and children. It is through faithfulness to these primary responsibilities that God equips women for success in her work.

That is why the last four principles explore those primary places in a woman's life: hospitality, marriage, motherhood, and, of course, the culmination of a wise woman's life as a matriarch.

In *hospitality*, we see the life-giving goodness of those who create real space in their homes and throughout their days for inconvenient, time-consuming, and holy hospitality. Jack loves to remind me that "the Christian hearth is our dinner table, which is the altar where we offer our songs, our prayers, and food, to the Lord in gratitude."

In *marriage on mission*, we explore the goodness of marriage as an asymmetrical union of man and woman, distinct in their creation and calling, yet forged together as battle-mates for a life of greatness and goodness. Such a vision of marriage, where the husband is the head of the wife and she is his glory, reflects the mystery of Christ and the Church (see Ephesians 5:21–33).

As *warrior mothers*, we devote ourselves wholeheartedly to the calling of motherhood, being open to life in marriage, and remaining faithful as spiritual mothers, especially if we are not married or are struggling with infertility. This principle does not deem women without children as less than; far from it. Instead, it explores the goodness of children in and of themselves and explores to the procreative potential inherent in being a woman.

Finally, as *wise women acting as counselors and negotiators*, we see the fruit and calling of matriarchs in the Bible, who disciple younger women and serve as examples in everything of what a well-lived and faithful life looks like: to love their husbands and children, to be self-controlled, pure, and kind, to be keepers of their homes, and to be submissive to their own husbands. Such glory shines brightly not by doing nothing or by replacing godly men, but by restoring godliness where it falters and helping younger women pursue wisdom and holiness.

I am not a wise matriarch yet, though Lord willing I will be one day. But I, like you, am on this journey and desire to grow into a wise and godly woman. This book has been my exploration of what the Bible teaches so that we can be equipped to find and follow the example of such godly women in our own lives.

The Dragon Today

Indeed, when we first met Satan, he appeared as a serpent in the book of Genesis. He slid quietly into the garden and spoke softly to the woman. His question was subtle enough to sound thoughtful and his deception close enough to the truth to sound believable. But that small deception opened the floodgates of sin. It fractured the peace of creation and ushered in the long story of rebellion and redemption that runs through the entire Bible.

And, just like women have the maiden, mother, and matriarch maturation arc, so the serpent matures throughout the Bible from a serpent to a fiery, roaring dragon seeking whom he may devour. In Revelation 12, we see Satan as a dragon: red, imposing, crowned with his own evil power, and raging against God's people. We cannot face a dragon with the naïveté of Eden. We cannot answer the flood of lies and pressures of our day with the same half-hearted responses that failed Eve. We need the wisdom of women who have matured into their calling. We need women who have trained their hearts and minds for battle. We need to become like Lady Wisdom in a world overrun with folly.

God has given us everything we need to stand firm, but we must learn how to use those tools: our union with Christ, the weapon of His Word, and knowing who our enemy is.

First, union.

Union with Christ means that we no longer build our lives on fragile foundations like career, reputation, or self-expression. It means we stop asking the question, "Who am I?" and start asking, "Who is He, and how has He called me to live?" It means that when lies about womanhood swirl around us, we can stand firm. We belong to Christ. We are loved, chosen, redeemed, and secure. No enemy can snatch us from His hand.

This union also reorients our purpose. We are not here to chase self-fulfillment or curate impressive résumés. We are here to glorify God and advance His kingdom. We are here to raise children in the fear of the Lord, to build homes that become outposts of heaven, to encourage our brothers in the faith, and to speak life in a hurting world. And we are here to do all of it, not in our own strength, but in His.

Second, our weapon.

Eve's fall did not come because the serpent overpowered her. It came because she laid down the only weapon that could have protected her: the Word of God. She listened to her own reasoning instead of His commands. And when she did, the serpent's lies found their mark.

We are given the same weapon today, and it is no less powerful. The Bible calls the Word of God "living and active, sharper than any two-edged sword" (Hebrews 4:12). It is the weapon that exposes falsehood, cuts through deception, and defends us against temptation. It is also the tool that shapes, corrects, and trains us for righteousness.

Too often, we leave this sword sheathed. We treat the Bible like an optional supplement to our faith rather than its foundation. We rely on Instagram devotionals or inspirational quotes instead of studying the Word deeply.

We cannot fight dragons with half-remembered verses. We cannot stand firm if we do not know what God has said. The Word must dwell richly in us, forming our convictions, guiding our decisions, and shaping our speech. We must read it, meditate on it, memorize it, pray it, and teach it. We must speak it over our homes and wield it against every lie that tries to root itself in our hearts. When we do, we are no longer easy prey. We become victorious over the enemy's plans.

Finally, we must know our enemy.

Our battle is not against flesh and blood. It is not against men or systems or even culture itself. It is against the spiritual forces of darkness that twist, distort, and destroy what God has made. It is against Satan, the father of lies.

When we are united with Christ, wield God's Word, and recognize God's enemy as our true enemy, we are "no longer [like] children, tossed to and fro by the waves and carried about by every wind of doctrine, by human cunning, by craftiness in deceitful schemes" (Ephesians 4:14).

That is my prayer for each of you.

> *Now to him who is able to do far more abundantly than all that we ask or think, according to the power at work within us, to him be glory in the church and in Christ Jesus throughout all generations, forever and ever. Amen.*
>
> —Ephesians 3:20–21

Acknowledgments

They say that writing a book is like a labor of love, and on many days, I almost would have preferred to be in twelve hours of labor again than deal with the arduous process of taking copious amounts of research and interesting (to me, at least) insights and weaving them into an engaging read. When preparing my book pitch, I somehow convinced myself that writing a book is just the sum of the effort of writing several essays. I write research essays for a living. How much harder could a book be? Harder. A lot harder.

As I wrestled with each sentence and Bible verse, I experienced the joy of applying oneself completely to a project and drawing forth new insights, precise descriptions, and greater mental discipline than ever before. Growing up, I wrote all the time: countless prayer journals, little stories for my younger siblings, poetry, and more. I told everyone I wanted to be a writer. It is surreal, to say the least, to publish this book in your hands. (Or, if you're like me and listen to books more than you read, in your ears.) To write is to think, and to share ideas is to enter into meaningful relationships with God, the past, and those around you. I would not have been able to do this work without the generous support of many people, and so without further ado, my acknowledgments:

First, I am deeply grateful to The Heritage Foundation for allowing me the work time to pursue this project. Without it, I never would have been able to write this book. I am so deeply indebted to my first director there, Dr. Jay Richards, who invested in me and my writing such that I am far more talented and readable than I would ever be otherwise.

Second, to the love of my life, Jackson Waters: he is my inspiration, my love, and my delight, and without him, this book would not be possible. His excitement first encouraged me to pursue these topics, and his deep and abiding love for God and the Bible continues to refine my work today. Oh, how I desire to grow into a wise, faithful, and fearless battle-mate who is afraid of no fearful thing in support of your calling, Jack. I took vows to "honor and obey" you, and it was the best decision of my life.

To our daughters, Elizabeth and Cordelia: you are the greatest gifts God has ever given me, and it is my honor and joy to grow with you as your mother. Y'all are my motivation, my joy, and a source of humbling refinement in my life. I fall more in love with you each day, and I cannot wait to see where the Lord takes you as wise, faithful, and strong women of faith.

Third, for the many people who helped review this book: to Jack, Mary Francis Devlin, Madeline Peltzer, Mary Wheeler, Sarah Weaver, and others who offered keen edits and feedback, especially Jonathan and Courtney White, without whose detailed and thorough feedback this book would be much, much worse.

I would not have had the time to write the book without the help of my own mother, Melissa. Her self-sacrificial willingness to drive twelve hours to stay with us, watch our daughters, and help maintain the house while I traveled or wrote during the day made all the difference. Our girls have always been her delight (and she the delight of our daughters). I do not take that for granted. Thank you, Mom.

Thank you to my dad, Jim, for his tireless hard work and provision. Your support made it possible for our family to thrive throughout the years.

Mothers-in-law get a bad rap, but mine has been such a dear friend and mentor to me. C. S. Lewis said it best: "Friendship, I have said, is born at the moment when one man says to another 'What! You too? I thought that no one but myself. . . .'"[1] To Annie, I have felt this for you all from the moment we met those many years ago in your home in Alexandria, Virginia. Thank you for your wisdom and intentionality and for raising the remarkable son who became my husband.

To Victor R. Scott, my youth group pastor in middle and high school, counselor throughout college and beyond, and friend to this day: I am so grateful for the unapologetic and deep teachings you gave us from such an early age. You brought the full weight and goodness of the Bible to bear on my young heart, and I am eternally in your debt.

To the many mentors, professors, and friends who have challenged me, shared your wisdom, and introduced me to many great books, thinkers, and ideas: it is an honor to walk this life with you.

And of course, last but certainly not least, I want to thank my agent, Jonathan Bronitsky, who took a chance on a first-time author, and my wonderful editor, Kathryn Riggs, for her patient edits, thoughtful feedback, and shared sympathy through teething, sleepless nights, and the adventure of newborn life. We each welcomed a baby within a few months of signing the contract, making this journey all the more memorable (or perhaps harder to remember).

About the Author

Emma Waters is a writer, speaker, and policy analyst whose life and work are rooted in the conviction that Jesus Christ is Lord over all. As a Policy Analyst in the Center for Technology and the Human Person at The Heritage Foundation, Emma explores the moral questions shaping our modern world: from family and biotechnology to the meaning of human dignity. Yet for her, this work is not merely intellectual; it is an act of discipleship.

Emma's mission is to bring the good news of Jesus Christ to bear on every aspect of our lives from our personal relationships and our call to faithful marriage and motherhood, to the public square where ideas about life and family take shape. She believes that when Christ's reign is recognized in our homes, our hearts, and our policies, human flourishing follows.

She graduated Valedictorian from Lee University with degrees in Political Science and Biblical & Theological Studies, and her writing and words have appeared in *First Things*, the *Wall Street Journal*, the *Washington Post*, the *New York Times*, *The Gospel Coalition*, *World Magazine*, *American Reformer*, *The Federalist*, *Newsweek*, *Fox News*, *RealClear Policy*, *The Daily Signal*, and more.

Emma is married to Jack, a postulant in the Anglican Church of North America and full-time seminary student at the time of this writing.

Together, they are joyfully raising their children and crafting a productive home economy where faith, family, and work flow from the home, rather than in isolation from it. They love to host, to travel, and to experience the world as a family, and would love to host you one day, too.

Emma has appeared, sometimes barefoot and very postpartum, on the cover of the *New York Times*, and has, at other times, spoken at the United Nations or briefed members of Congress. It's all about balance, right? But most days come down to a slow yet diligent commitment to care for the girls, manage the home, extend hospitality, and go on as many walks as possible. She holds all these moments side by side as a testament to God's grace in every season of life.

There are few things that bring her more delight than seeing the world through the eyes of her children and helping others see that the gospel transforms every corner of life.

Follow her work on X @emlwaters.

Notes

Preface

1 C. S. Lewis, *The Collected Letters of C. S. Lewis, Vol. III, Narnia, Cambridge and Joy, 1950–1963,* ed. Walter Hooper (San Francisco: Harper San Francisco, 2007), 111.

Introduction

1 Elana Schor, "So, Did the 'Year of the Woman' Really Change Anything?" *Politico*, December 10, 2019, https://www.politico.com/news/magazine/2019/12/10/women-politics-congress-2020-075460. In 2017, *Politico* also published a piece predicting "Why 2020 will be the year of the woman."

2 Ivana Greco, "Reframing Family Policy," *National Affairs*, no. 65 (Fall 2022), https://nationalaffairs.com/publications/detail/reframing-family-policy.

3 Danielle Kurtzleben, "A Record Number of Women Will Serve in Congress, With Potentially More to Come," NPR, November 7, 2018, https://www.npr.org/2018/11/07/665019211/a-record-number-of-women-will-serve-in-congress-with-potentially-more-to-come.

4 Jenny Gold, "The Women's Health Issue No One Talks About," *PBS NewsHour*, Kaiser Health News, https://www.pbs.org/newshour/health/womens-health-issue-no-one-talks.

5 Lea Winerman, "By the Numbers: Antidepressant Use on the Rise," *Monitor on Psychology* 48, no. 10 (November 2017): 120, https://www.apa.org/monitor/2017/11/numbers.

6 Laura A. Pratt, Debra J. Brody, and Qiuping Gu, "Antidepressant Use Among Persons Aged 12 and Over: United States, 2011–2014," NCHS Data Brief, no. 283 (Hyattsville, MD: National Center for Health Statistics, Centers for Disease Control and Prevention, August 2017), https://www.cdc.gov/nchs/products/databriefs/db283.htm.

7 Jenny Gold, "The Women's Health Issue No One Talks About," *PBS NewsHour*, Kaiser Health News, https://www.pbs.org/newshour/health/womens-health-issue-no-one-talks.

8 Carolina Aragão, "Among Young Adults Without Children, Men Are More Likely Than Women to Say They Want to Be Parents Someday," Pew Research Center, February 15, 2024, https://www.pewresearch.org/short-reads/2024/02/15/among-young-adults-without-children-men-are-more-likely-than-women-to-say-they-want-to-be-parents-someday.

9 Juliana Menasce Horowitz, Nikki Graf, and Gretchen Livingston, "Marriage and Cohabitation in the U.S.," Pew Research Center, November 6, 2019, https://www.pewresearch.org/social-trends/2019/11/06/marriage-and-cohabitation-in-the-u-s.

10 Mike Stobbe, "US Fertility Drops to New Low in 2024, CDC Data Shows," AP News, updated July 24, 2025, https://apnews.com/article/fertility-rate-us-low-cdc-replacement-532c4f43f420f29b32212db9cfa0e0af, accessed October 13, 2025.

11 James L. McQuivey, "To Have Kids or Not: Which Decision Do Americans Regret More?" Institute for Family Studies, June 10, 2021, https://ifstudies.org/blog/to-have-kids-or-not-which-decision-do-americans-regret-more.

12 Hadley Freeman, "'Tradwives': The New Trend for Submissive Women Has a Dark Heart and History," *The Guardian*, January 27, 2020, https://www.theguardian.com/fashion/2020/jan/27/tradwives-new-trend-submissive-women-dark-heart-history; Lauren Bravo, "Help! Am I Becoming an Accidental #TradWife?," *Refinery29*, April 21, 2020, https://www.refinery29.com/en-gb/help-ive-become-an-accidental-tradwife; Sophie Elmhirst, "The Rise and Fall of the Trad Wife," *The New Yorker*, March 29, 2024, https://www.newyorker.com/culture/persons-of-interest/the-rise-and-fall-of-the-trad-wife.

13 Brittany Hugoboom, "Hell Hath No Fury Like a Feminist Witnessing a Beautiful Woman Living Her Dreams," *Washington Examiner*, December 7, 2024, https://www.washingtonexaminer.com/opinion/3252757/hell-hath-no-fury-like-a-feminist-witnessing-a-beautiful-woman-living-her-dreams.

14 Dionne Searcy, "Was the Trump Election a Setback for Women? Even Women Do Not Agree," *New York Times*, November 12, 2024, https://www.nytimes.com/2024/11/12/us/elections/women-feminism-harris-trump.html.

15 Betty Friedan, *The Feminine Mystique* (New York: W. W. Norton, 1963), 15.

16 Mary Harrington, "Why Tradwives Aren't Trad Enough," *UnHerd*, January 30, 2020, https://unherd.com/2020/01/why-tradwife-just-isnt-trad-enough.

17 Ibid.

18 Lydia Saad, "Children a Key Factor in Women's Desire to Work Outside the Home," Gallup, October 7, 2015, https://news.gallup.com/poll/185674/children-key-factor-women-desire-work-outside-home.aspx.

19 American Compass survey, "American Compass, Home Building Survey Part II: Supporting Families," American Compass, February 2021, https://americancompass.org/home-building-survey-part-2/; James L. McQuivey, "New Book Offers Advice to Young Career Women Who Want More," Institute for Family Studies, April 15, 2024, https://ifstudies.org/blog/new-book-offers-advice-to-young-career-women-who-want-more.

20 US Bureau of Labor Statistics, "Employment Characteristics of Families—2024," News Release, April 23, 2025, https://www.bls.gov/news.release/pdf/famee.pdf.

21 Carrie Battan, "How Lucky Blue and Nara Aziza Smith Made Viral Internet Fame from Scratch," *GQ*, August 7, 2024, https://www.gq.com/story/lucky-blue-nara-aziza-smith-gq-hype.

22 Marc Trussler and Stephanie Perry, "Poll: Gen Z's Gender Divide Reaches Beyond Politics and Into Its Views on Marriage, Children and Success," NBC News, September 8, 2025, https://www.nbcnews.com/politics/politics-news/poll-gen-zs-gender-divide-reaches-politics-views-marriage-children-suc-rcna229255.

23 Ibid.

24 Ibid.

25 One Passion One Devotion, "Jael—Unsung Hero," May 31, 2022, https://onepassiononedevotion.wordpress.com/2022/05/31/jael-unsung-hero.

26 James B. Jordan, "Introduction to Biblical Theology," Theopolis Institute, https://theopolisinstitute.com/wp-content/uploads/edd/2015/11/Introduction-to-Biblical-Theology.-By-James-Jordan.pdf, accessed October 13, 2025.

27 Ibid.

Principle One

1 Marshall McLuhan and Quentin Fiore, *The Medium Is the Massage: An Inventory of Effects* (New York: Bantam Books, 1967).

2 David J. Ayers, "Cohabitation Among Evangelicals: A New Norm?" Institute for Family Studies, April 19, 2021, https://ifstudies.org/blog/cohabitation-among-evangelicals-a-new-norm.

3 Allie Beth Stuckey, *Toxic Empathy: How Progressives Exploit Christian Compassion* (New York: Sentinel, 2024), xiii.

4 Ibid., 43.

5 This quote has been widely attributed to Jim Wilson, but I don't have a citation for it.

Principle Two

1 Elisabeth Elliot, *A Chance to Die: The Life and Legacy of Amy Carmichael* (Grand Rapids: Revell, 2005), 167.

2 Amy Carmichael, *Gold Cord: The Story of a Fellowship* (London: SPCK, 1932), 22.

3 Ibid., 22.

4 Ibid., 84.

5 Ibid.

6 Aaron M. Renn, *Life in the Negative World: Confronting Challenges in an Anti-Christian Culture* (Zondervan, 2024).

7 Erin El Issa, "Women and Credit Through the Decades: The 1970s," *NerdWallet*, May 17, 2023, https://www.nerdwallet.com/article/credit-cards/women-credit-decades-70s.

8 James B. Jordan, *Primeval Saints: Studies in the Patriarchs of Genesis* (Moscow, ID: Canon Press, 2001), 95.

9 Liz Abrams, "God's Children Are Not for Sale: *Sound of Freedom* Sheds Light on the Evil of Child Trafficking," Answers in Genesis, July 19, 2023, https://answersingenesis.org/reviews/movies/gods-children-are-not-for-sale/?srsltid=AfmBOoqZkulwvIDO6OsDN5Zz7ETfmMpTE83zrrEC4kWdnXUJtxKnTNY7.

10 Soraya Chemaly, *Rage Becomes Her: The Power of Women's Anger* (New York: Atria Books, 2018), 295.

11 Brittney Cooper, "The Problem with Sass," in *The Portable Feminist Reader*, ed. Roxane Gay (New York: Penguin Books, 2025), 294, Kindle edition.

12 Pat Mitchell, "The Transformative Power of Women's Anger," *Ms. Magazine*, September 21, 2018, https://msmagazine.com/2018/09/21/transformative-power-womens-anger.

13 Hailey E. Murphy, "A Lack of Understanding: Unpacking the Transformative Power of Women's Anger in Politics," *Women's Studies International Forum* 107 (November–December 2024): 102996, https://doi.org/10.1016/j.wsif.2024.102996.

14 Leah Hall, *Fear and Anger at Retrieval Impact Memory Performance*, Clark Honors College thesis, University of Oregon, 2024, https://scholarsbank.uoregon.edu/items/f5174f8a-bf4f-4057-b3a8-811e9b4add29.

15 Philip A. Gable et al., "Anger Perceptually and Conceptually Narrows Cognitive Scope," *Journal of Personality and Social Psychology* 109, no. 1 (2015): 163–74, https://doi.org/10.1037/a0039226.

16 Jutta Lindert et al., "Depression-, Anxiety-, and Anger and Cognitive Functions: Findings from a Longitudinal Prospective Study," *Frontiers in Psychiatry* 12 (2021): Article 665742, https://doi.org/10.3389/fpsyt.2021.665742.

17 Yoichi Chida and Andrew Steptoe, "The Association of Anger and Hostility with Future Coronary Heart Disease: A Meta-Analytic Review of Prospective Evidence," *JACC*, 53, no. 11 (March 2009): 936–46, https://doi.org/10.1016/j.jacc.2008.11.044.

18 Mayumi Okuda et al., "Prevalence and Correlates of Anger in the Community: Results from a National Survey," *CNS Spectrums* 20, no. 2 (April 2015): 130–39, https://doi.org/10.1017/S1092852914000182.

Principle Three

1 Congressional Research Service, *The Equal Rights Amendment: Background and Recent Legal Developments,* CRS Report No. R47619 (Washington, DC: Congress.gov, accessed October 20, 2025), https://www.congress.gov/crs-product/R47619.

2 Abigail Dodds, "Is Jael a Model Woman? Feminine Fight in a Feminist Age," *Desiring God*, July 2, 2022, https://www.desiringgod.org/articles/is-jael-a-model-woman.

3 One Passion One Devotion, "Jael—Unsung Hero," May 31, 2022, https://onepassiononedevotion.wordpress.com/2022/05/31/jael-unsung-hero.

4 Joe Rigney, *The Sin of Empathy: Compassion and Its Counterfeits* (Moscow, ID: Canon Press, 2025), 140–41, Kindle edition.

5 Martin Luther, *The Martin Luther Christmas Book*, ed. and trans. Roland H. Bainton (Philadelphia: Westminster Press, 1948), 22, https://archive.org/details/martinlutherchri0000luth.

6 Pamela Paul, "The Conservative Women Who Are 'Having It All,'" *Wall Street Journal*, August 1, 2025, https://www.wsj.com/lifestyle/relationships/the-conservative-women-who-are-having-it-all-84077b73.

Principle Four

1 I am indebted to Yoram Hazony's thoughtful *God and Politics in Esther* for my own understanding of the text. Yoram Hazony, *God and Politics in Esther*, 2nd ed. (Cambridge: Cambridge University Press, 2015).

2 Mark Brians II and Drew A. Knowles, *Hospitality: The Convivial Mission of God* (Birmingham, AL: Athanasius Press, 2024), 8, Kindle edition. I am indebted to this excellent book for providing a strong basis for my biblical theology of hospitality throughout this chapter.

3 "God invited us to a meal, and we rejected the meal and ate instead with the Accuser, the Satan. The hospitable welcome of our creation was forsaken when guest rose up against the Host of Life." Ibid., 30.

4 NPR Staff, "Fire, Water, Air, Earth: Michael Pollan Gets Elemental in *Cooked*," NPR, April 21, 2013, https://www.npr.org/2013/04/21/177501735/fire-water-air-earth-michael-pollan-gets-elemental-in-cooked.

5 Ibid.

6 Marshall McLuhan, *Understanding Media: The Extensions of Man* (New York: McGraw-Hill, 1964).

7 Casey Means @CaseyMeansMD, X post, February 19, 2024, https://x.com/CaseyMeansMD/status/1759690337495531700.

8 James B. Jordan, *Introduction to Biblical Theology* (Theopolis Institute PDF), 16 https://theopolisinstitute.com/wp-content/uploads/edd/2015/11/Introduction-to-Biblical-Theology.-By-James-Jordan.pdf, accessed October 13, 2025.

9 Mark Brians and Drew A. Knowles, *Hospitality: The Convivial Mission of God* (Birmingham: Athanasius Press, 2024), 16, Kindle edition.

Principle Five

1 Joseph Campbell, *The Hero with a Thousand Faces* (Novato, CA: New World Library, 2008).

2 Evan Smith, "Quest for a Female Story Model," *Script Magazine*, August 23, 2022, https://scriptmag.com/screenplays/quest-for-a-female-story-model. From a Joseph Campbell quote in 1981—repeated so often it is part of the lore.

3 Maureen Murdock, *The Heroine's Journey: Woman's Quest for Wholeness* (Boston: Shambhala Publications, 1990).

4 Maureen Murdock, "The Heroine's Journey," in *Encyclopedia of Psychology and Religion*, ed. David A. Leeming (Springer, 2016), https://maureenmurdock.com/articles/articles-the-heroines-journey.

5 I draw heavily from Peter Leithart's *The Glory of Man* for this section and am gratefully indebted to him for such an excellent book and pivotal insight. Peter J. Leithart, *The Glory of Man* (Birmingham, AL: Theopolis Books, 2024).

6 Ibid., 77, Kindle edition.

7 Ibid., 79.

8 Ibid.,80.

9 Ibid., 71. This phrase, to my knowledge, was first used by Leithart in this book.

10 Matthew Henry, *Matthew Henry Commentary on the Whole Bible (Complete)*, Vol. 1, *Genesis to Deuteronomy* (n.p., 1706), http://www.biblestudytools.com/ commentaries/matthew-henry-complete/genesis.

11 *The Glory of Man*, 137.

12 Ibid., 139.

13 This pithy reference comes from Rosaria Butterfield, author of *Five Lies of Our Anti-Christian Age*, when speaking at the Center for Christian Virtue Essential Summit in Columbus, Ohio, on October 2, 2025. This is a paraphrase from her remarks.

14 *The Glory of Man*, 80.

15 Ibid., 81.

16 Arthur Aron et al., "The Experimental Generation of Interpersonal Closeness: A Procedure and Some Preliminary Findings," *Personality and Social Psychology Bulletin* 23, no. 4 (April 1997): 363–77, https://journals.sagepub.com/doi/pdf/10.1177/0146167297234003.

17 Megan Basham, *Beside Every Successful Man: A Woman's Guide to Having It All* (Centerport: Forum Books, 2008).

18 John Van Epp, *How to Avoid Falling in Love with a Jerk* (New York: McGraw Hill, 2008), online summary bullet points from Amazon.

19 Catherine Allgor, *Parlor Politics: In Which the Ladies of Washington Help Build a City and a Government* (Charlottesville: University of Virginia Press, 2000), 83.

Principle Six

1 Suzanne Blake, "Most Parents Are Going Into Debt to Provide for Their Kids: Study," *Newsweek*, August 25, 2025, https://www.newsweek.com/most-parents-going-debt-provide-kids-2118978; Jennifer Fawcett, "Nobody Warns You About the Identity Crisis of Motherhood," *Oprah Daily*, September 25, 2025, https://www.oprahdaily.com/life/wholeness/a66289319/motherhood-identity-loss; Sarah Green Carmichael, "The New Work-Life Balance: Don't Have Kids," *Bloomberg*, February 4, 2024, https://www.bloomberg.com/opinion/articles/2024-02-04/career-demands-meager-leave-policies-drive-down-birth-rate; Catherine Deveny, "Sorry, but Being a Mother Is Not the Most Important Job in the World," *The Guardian*, November 18, 2013, https://www.theguardian.com/commentisfree/2013/nov/18/sorry-but-being-a-mother-is-not-the-most-important-job-in-the-world; Ellen Walker, "Should Women Be Freed from the Motherhood Mandate?" *Psychology Today*, December 15, 2014, https://www.psychologytoday.com/us/blog/complete-without-kids/201412/should-women-be-freed-the-motherhood-mandate; Lara Bazelon, "Divorce Can Be an Act of Radical Self-Love," *New York Times*, September 30, 2021, https://www.nytimes.com/2021/09/30/opinion/divorce-children.html; Travis Rieder, "Science Proves Kids Are Bad for Earth. Morality Suggests We Stop Having Them," *NBC News*, November 15, 2017, https://www.nbcnews.com/think/opinion/science-proves-kids-are-bad-earth-morality-suggests-we-stop-ncna821121.

2 Kim Ward, "MSU Study Confirms: 1 in 5 Adults Don't Want Children—and They Don't Regret It Later," *Michigan State University Department of Psychology News*, April 5, 2023, https://psychology.msu.edu/news-events/news/archives/2023/childfree-study-confirmed-april2023.html.

3 The Harris Poll, "Personal Independence Behind Declining Birth Rates," October 11, 2022, https://theharrispoll.com/personal-independence-behind-declining-birth-rates.

4 *The Harris Poll,* "Personal Independence Behind Declining Birth Rates," *Brief*, October 11, 2022, https://theharrispoll.com/briefs/birth-rates/.

5 Marc Trussler and Stephanie Perry, "Poll: Gen Z's Gender Divide Reaches Beyond Politics and Into Its Views on Marriage, Children and Success," *NBC News*, September 8, 2025, https://www.nbcnews.com/

politics/politics-news/poll-gen-zs-gender-divide-reaches-politics-views-marriage-children-suc-rcna229255.

6 Mike Stobbe, "The US Fertility Rate Reached a New Low in 2024, CDC Data Shows," AP News, updated July 24, 2025, https://apnews.com/article/us-fertility-rate-2024-cdc-data-5b0b1b22dfb24b25a7b8cbe7fbe3a4ac.

7 The White House, "Fact Sheet: President Donald J. Trump Announces Actions to Lower Costs and Expand Access to In Vitro Fertilization (IVF) and High-Quality Fertility Care," October 16, 2025, https://www.whitehouse.gov/fact-sheets/2025/10/fact-sheet-president-donald-j-trump-announces-actions-to-lower-costs-and-expand-access-to-in-vitro-fertilization-ivf-and-high-quality-fertility-care.

8 Monica Hesse, "Don't Pin the Birth Rate Problem on the Birth Givers," *Washington Post*, June 26, 2024, https://www.washingtonpost.com/style/power/2024/06/26/birth-rate-blame-game.

9 Brad Wilcox and Wendy Wang, "Who Is Happiest? Married Mothers and Fathers, Per the Latest General Social Survey," Institute for Family Studies, September 12, 2023, https://ifstudies.org/blog/who-is-happiest-married-mothers-and-fathers-per-the-latest-general-social-survey. Based on the 2022 General Social Survey (GSS) data in the United States.

10 Jean M. Twenge, Jenet Erickson, Wendy Wang, and Brad Wilcox, *In Pursuit: Marriage, Motherhood, and Women's Well-Being* (Charlottesville: Institute for Family Studies, August 2025), https://ifstudies.org/report-brief/in-pursuit-marriage-motherhood-and-womens-well-being.

11 This section on Genesis 12–25 relies on the CEB translation of the Bible.

12 Erica Komisar, "We Need a New Feminism That Embraces Motherhood as Meaningful Work," Institute for Family Studies, October 15, 2024, https://ifstudies.org/blog/we-need-new-feminism-that-embraces-motherhood-as-meaningful-work.

13 Ibid.

14 Barbara S. Kisilevsky et al., "Effects of Experience on Fetal Voice Recognition." *Psychological Science* 14, no. 3 (2003): 220–24; Benoist Schaal, Ilona Marlier, and Robert Soussignan, "Human Foetuses Learn Odours from Their Pregnant Mother's Diet." *Chemical Senses* 25, no. 6 (2000): 729–37; K. Mizuno, N. Mizuno, T. Shinohara, and M. Noda, "Mother-Infant Skin-to-Skin Contact After Delivery Results in Early Recognition of Own Mother's Milk Odour," *Acta Paediatrica* 93, no. 12

(December 2004): 1640–45, https://doi.org/10.1080/08035250410023115; S. Wagner, S. Issanchou, C. Chabanet, C. Lange, B. Schaal, and S. Monnery-Patris, "Weanling Infants Prefer the Odors of Green Vegetables, Cheese, and Fish When Their Mothers Consumed These Foods During Pregnancy and/or Lactation," *Chemical Senses* 44, no. 4 (April 15, 2019): 257–65, https://doi.org/10.1093/chemse/bjz011.

15 Myron A. Hofer, "Hidden Regulators in Attachment, Separation, and Loss," in *Attachment Theory: Social, Developmental, and Clinical Perspectives,* ed. J. Cassidy and P. R. Shaver (New York: Guilford Press, 2008), 203–30.

16 Kerstin Uvnäs Moberg and Maria Prime, "Oxytocin Effects in Mothers and Infants During Breastfeeding," *Infant* 6, no. 6 (2010): 201–6; Ruth Feldman, Ilanit Gordon, and Orna Zagoory-Sharon, "Maternal and Paternal Plasma, Salivary, and Urinary Oxytocin and Parent–Infant Synchrony: Considering Stress and Affiliation Components of Human Bonding," *Developmental Science* 14, no. 4 (2011): 752–61, https://doi.org/10.1111/j.1467-7687.2010.01021.x; Leslie J. Seltzer, Ashley R. Prososki, Toni E. Ziegler, and Seth D. Pollak, "Instant Messages vs. Speech: Hormones and Why We Still Need to Hear Each Other," *Evolution and Human Behavior* 33, no. 1 (January 2012): 42–45, https://doi.org/10.1016/j.evolhumbehav.2011.05.004.

17 Karin Grossmann et al., "The Uniqueness of the Child–Father Attachment Relationship: Fathers' Sensitive and Challenging Play as a Pivotal Variable in a 16-Year Longitudinal Study," *Social Development* 11, no. 3 (2002): 307–31, https://doi.org/10.1111/1467-9507.00202.

18 S. Madigan et al., "The First 20,000 Strange Situation Procedures: A Meta-Analytic Review," *Psychological Bulletin,* 149(1–2), 99–132, https://doi.org/10.1037/bul0000388. I first came across this study on Erica Komisar's Substack: https://ericakomisar.substack.com/p/why-marriage-still-brightens-many.

19 Kathryn A. Kerns and Laura E. Brumariu, "Is Insecure Parent–Child Attachment a Risk Factor for the Development of Anxiety in Childhood or Adolescence?" *Child Development Perspectives* 8, no. 1 (2014): 12–17, https://pmc.ncbi.nlm.nih.gov/articles/PMC3960076; NSPCC Learning, "Attachment and Child Development," accessed October 20, 2025, https://learning.nspcc.org.uk/child-health-development/attachment-early-years; Positive Psychology, "Disorganized Attachment

Style: Everything You Need to Know," May 10, 2024, https://positivepsychology.com/disorganized-attachment/.

20 Jenet Erickson and Jay Belsky, "Another Perspective on the Latest Research on Early Child Care," Institute for Family Studies, September 27, 2023, https://ifstudies.org/blog/another-perspective-on-the-latest-research-on-early-child-care. The authors discuss the "NICHD Study of Early Child Care and Youth Development (NICHD-SECC), which followed 1,300 children from birth to age 15. . . . The earliest findings indicated that at 15 months of age, more time spent in any kind of child care was associated with an increased risk of insecure infant-mother attachment relationship for some children. By 24 months of age, more time in child care across the first 2 years predicted less social competence and cooperation, and more caregiver-reported behavior problems. By age 3, these negative effects seemed to disappear. One of us who was involved in the study acknowledged that the age-3 findings showing no negative effects were potentially important, but only if they continued as children developed. Unfortunately, they did not." They go on to summarize the study, saying, "The negative outcomes associated with early and extensive hours in child care persisted into the assessments done in kindergarten, first, third and sixth grades, as well as during adolescence. By third grade, children who had experienced more cumulative hours of child care across their first 4.5 years of life were at increased risk for fewer social skills, poorer work habits, problem behaviors, and teacher conflict, especially if they had been in day care centers. By the sixth grade, quantity of time in day care centers continued to predict problem behaviors, even if teacher-child conflict, social skills, and work habits no longer proved to be associated with quantity of care. At age 15, more hours in a day care centers predicted significantly more problem behaviors, risk taking (including using alcohol, tobacco, and other drugs), and impulsivity in participating in unsafe activities."

21 Erica Komisar, "Government Policy Should Enable Mothers to Care for Their Young Children at Home," Institute for Family Studies, January 11, 2024, https://ifstudies.org/blog/government-policy-should-enable-mothers-to-care-for-their-young-children-at-home.

22 Kristin Nystad et al., "Toddlers' Stress During Transition to Childcare," *European Early Childhood Education Research Journal* 29 (2021): 1–26, https://doi.org/10.1080/1350293X.2021.1895269.

23 James E. Swain, et al.,"Approaching the Biology of Human Parental Attachment: Brain Imaging, Oxytocin and Coordinated Assessments of Mothers and Fathers," *Brain Research* 1580 (2014): 78–101, https://doi.org/10.1016/j.brainres.2014.03.007; Pilyoung Kim et al., "The Maternal Brain and Its Plasticity in Humans," *Hormones and Behavior* 77 (2016): 113–123, https://doi.org/10.1016/j.yhbeh.2015.08.001.

24 Ruth Feldman, "The Adaptive Human Parental Brain: Implications for Children's Social Development," *Trends in Neurosciences* 38, no. 6 (2015): 387–99, https://doi.org/10.1016/j.tins.2015.04.004.

25 Lane Strathearn et al., "What's in a Smile? Maternal Brain Responses to Infant Facial Cues," *Pediatrics* 122, no. 1 (2008): 40–51, https://doi.org/10.1542/peds.2007-1566.

26 Eyal Abraham et al., "Father's Brain Is Sensitive to Childcare Experiences," *Proceedings of the National Academy of Sciences* 111, no. 27 (2014): 9792–97, https://doi.org/10.1073/pnas.1402569111; Pilyoung Kim et al., "Neural Plasticity in Fathers of Human Infants," *Social Neuroscience* 9, no. 5 (October 2014): 522–35, https://doi.org/10.1080/17470919.2014.933713.

27 Clare Morell, "Don't Just Say Motherhood Matters, Prove It with Your Life," *The Federalist*, January 26, 2022. https://thefederalist.com/2022/01/26/dont-just-say-motherhood-matters-prove-it-with-your-life.

28 Erica Komisar, *Being There: Raising Resilient Children* (ARC Research Paper, 2023), https://static1.squarespace.com/static/6516e3215981fa376a3ea80d/t/653667f5acfe264c1f79f3bf/1698064392580/Being+There%3A+Raising+Resilient+Children+-+Erica+Komisar+-+ARC+Research+Paper.

29 Nassim Nicholas Taleb, *Antifragile: Things That Gain from Disorder* (New York: Random House, 2012).

30 Centers for Disease Control and Prevention, "National Survey of Family Growth—I Listing," National Center for Health Statistics, updated December 16, 2022, https://www.cdc.gov/nchs/nsfg/key_statistics/i-keystat.htm.

31 International Institute for Restorative Reproductive Medicine, "What Is RRM?" International Institute for Restorative Reproductive Medicine, accessed October 30, 2025, https://iirrm.org/what-is-rrm.

32 Emma Waters, "Why the IVF Industry Must Be Regulated," The Heritage Foundation, July 11, 2023, https://www.heritage.org/life/report/why-the-ivf-industry-must-be-regulated.

33 Ibid.

34 Saswati Sunderam et al., "Assisted Reproductive Technology Surveillance—United States, 2018," *MMWR Surveill Summ* 2022; 71 (No. 4): 1–19; M. Vaajala et al., "In Vitro Fertilization Increases the Odds of Gestational Diabetes: A Nationwide Register-Based Cohort Study," *Acta Diabetologica* 60, no. 2 (2023): 319–21, https://doi.org/10.1007/s00592-022-01975-z; Klaus Fiedler and Daniel Ezcurra, "Predicting and Preventing Ovarian Hyperstimulation Syndrome (OHSS): The Need for Individualized Not Standardized Treatment," *Reproductive Biology and Endocrinology* 10 (2012): 32, https://doi.org/10.1186/1477-7827-10-32; Evangelia Antoniou et al., "The Kind of Conception Affects the Kind of Cesarean Delivery in Primiparous Women," *Mater Sociomed* 33, no. 3 (September 2021): 188–94, https://doi.org/10.5455/msm.2021.33.188-194; Reza Omani-Samani et al., "Risk of Preeclampsia Following Assisted Reproductive Technology: Systematic Review and Meta-Analysis of 72 Cohort Studies," *Journal of Maternal-Fetal & Neonatal Medicine* 33 (16): 2826–40, doi:10.1080/14767058.2018.1560406; L. L. Lei et al., "Perinatal Complications and Live-Birth Outcomes Following Assisted Reproductive Technology: A Retrospective Cohort Study," *Chinese Medical Journal* 132, no. 20 (2019): 2408–16, https://doi.org/10.1097/CM9.0000000000000484.

35 S. L. Boulet et al., "Assisted Reproductive Technology and Birth Defects Among Liveborn Infants in Florida, Massachusetts, and Michigan, 2000–2010," *JAMA Pediatrics* 170, no. 6 (2016): e154934, https://doi.org/10.1001/jamapediatrics.2015.4934; Ying Liang et al., "Which Type of Congenital Malformations Is Significantly Increased in Singleton Pregnancies Following After In Vitro Fertilization/Intracytoplasmic Sperm Injection: A Systematic Review and Meta-Analysis," *Oncotarget* 9, no. 3 (December 25, 2017): 4267–78, https://doi.org/10.18632/oncotarget.23689; Sine Berntsen et al., "A Systematic Review and Meta-Analysis on the Association Between ICSI and Chromosome Abnormalities," *Human Reproduction Update* 27, no. 5 (September–October 2021): 801–47, https://doi.org/10.1093/humupd/dmab005; Matthew J. Maenner et al., "Prevalence and Characteristics of Autism Spectrum Disorder Among Children Aged 8 Years—Autism and Developmental Disabilities Monitoring Network,

11 Sites, United States, 2020," *MMWR Surveillance Summaries* 72, no. SS-2 (2023): 1–14, https://doi.org/10.15585/mmwr.ss7202a1; M. Hargreave, "Fertility Treatment and Childhood Cancer Risk," *JAMA Network Open* 5, no. 8 (2022): e2230162, https://doi.org/10.1001/jamanetworkopen.2022.30162; M. Veeramani et al., "Assisted Reproduction and Congenital Malformations: A Systematic Review and Meta-Analysis," *Congenit Anom* (Kyoto) 2024; 64(3):107–15, doi:10.1111/cga.12561; J. A. Gingold et al., "Comparing Reproductive Outcomes Between Conventional In Vitro Fertilization and Nonindicated Intracytoplasmic Sperm Injection in Autologous Embryo Transfer Cycles: A Society for Assisted Reproductive Technology Clinic Outcome Reporting System Study," *F&S Rep.* 2021; 5(1):23–32, doi:10.1016/j.xfre.2020.10.003.

36 Joseph B. Stanford and Ken R. Smith, "Natural Procreative Technology for Infertility and Recurrent Miscarriage: Outcomes in a Contemporary Cohort." *Journal of the American Board of Family Medicine* 21, no. 5: 375–84, https://www.jabfm.org/content/jabfp/21/5/375.full.pdf; P. Frank-Herrmann et al., "Natural Conception Rates in Subfertile Couples Following Fertility Awareness Training," *Archives of Gynecology and Obstetrics* 295 (2017): 1015–24, https://doi.org/10.1007/s00404-017-4294-z; Phil C. Boyle et al., "Healthy Singleton Pregnancies from Restorative Reproductive Medicine (RRM) After Failed IVF," *Frontiers in Medicine,* 5, no. 210 (July 31, 2018): https://pmc.ncbi.nlm.nih.gov/articles/PMC6079215/; Phil Boyle et al., "Restorative Reproductive Medicine (RRM) Outcomes Compared to In-Vitro Fertilization (IVF) for the Treatment of Infertility: a Retrospective Evaluation of a 2019 Clinic Cohort Compared to One Cycle of IVF," *Journal of Restorative Reproductive Medicine* 1 (September 2025): https://doi.org/10.63264/gejytw70; Joseph Stanford et al., "International Natural Procreative Technology Evaluation and Surveillance of Treatment for Subfertility (iNEST): Enrollment and Methods," *Human Reproduction Open* 3 (2022): 1–15, https://doi.org/10.1093/hropen/hoac033.

37 Mohammad Reza Sadeghi, "Unexplained Infertility, the Controversial Matter in Management of Infertile Couples," *Journal of Reproduction & Infertility* 16, no. 1 (2015): 1–2.

38 I quote this TikTok video in my article: Emma Waters, "Let's Change How We Talk About Motherhood and Pregnancy," *Newsweek*, May 14, 2023, https://www.newsweek.com/lets-change-how-we-talk

-about-motherhood-pregnancy-opinion-1799828. You can find the original video here: motivationalmusee, TikTok, March 26, 2023, https://www.tiktok.com/@motivationalmusee/video/72149016056 13800709?is_from_webapp=1&sender_device=pc.

Principle Seven

1 IL House GOP, "Rep. Miller Acknowledges His Wife for Women's History Month," YouTube video, March 26, 2025, https://youtu.be/5FvD 63wBUWs?si=wUbxEFsVuHDflaPH.

2 James B. Jordan, "Introduction to Biblical Theology," Theopolis Institute, https://theopolisinstitute.com/wp-content/uploads/edd/2015/11 /Introduction-to-Biblical-Theology.-By-James-Jordan.pdf, accessed October 13, 2025, pg. 14.

3 Elisabeth Elliot, *Let Me Be a Woman: Notes on Womanhood for Valerie* (Wheaton, IL: Tyndale House Publishers, 1976), 45.

4 Anne-Marie Slaughter, "Why Women Still Can't Have It All," *The Atlantic*, August 15, 2012, https://www.theatlantic.com/magazine /archive/2012/07/why-women-still-cant-have-it-all/309020.

5 Abraham Kuyper, "Sphere Sovereignty," trans. George Kamp (public address at the inauguration of the Free University, Amsterdam, October 20, 1880), https://sources.neocalvinism.org/.full_pdfs/kuyper /SphereSovereignty_English.pdf.

6 James Edward McGoldrick, *God's Renaissance Man: Abraham Kuyper* (Darlington: Evangelical Press, 2000), 36.

7 Ibid., 37.

8 Patricia Patnode, "Soft Occultism," *The American Mind* (Claremont Institute), December 1, 2023, https://americanmind.org/salvo/soft -occultism.

9 Abigail Shrier, *Bad Therapy: Why the Kids Aren't Growing Up* (New York: Sentinel, 2024).

10 Barna Group, "*Gen Z* Women Struggle to Find Their Place in Christian Faith and Community," *Church Generations*, October 14, 2025, https://www.barna.com/trends/gen-z-women-struggling-in-faith.

11 Ibid.

12 Ibid.

Conclusion

1 John Stonestreet and Shane Morris, "Young Men Are Returning to Church," *Breakpoint*, July 9, 2025, https://colsoncenter.org/breakpoint/young-men-are-returning-to-church.

2 Brigham Tomco, "How Charlie Kirk Became 'Too Big to Ignore': Charlie Kirk Wants to Save Western Civilization. But Can He Win at Home?" *Deseret News*, September 7, 2025, https://www.deseret.com/politics/2025/09/07/charlie-kirk-on-faith-politics-and-his-plans-to-change-the-nation/.

3 Collin Rugg (@CollinRugg), "Charlie Kirk on how he wanted to be remembered. Question: 'How would you wanna be remembered?' Charlie: 'I wanna be remembered for courage for my faith. That that would be the most important thing. The most important thing is my faith in my life.'" *X* (formerly Twitter), September 10, 2025, last edited 11:03 p.m., https://x.com/CollinRugg/status/1965974414748692572.

4 Charlie Kirk (@charliekirk11), "Jesus defeated death so you can live," *X (*formerly Twitter), September 6, 2025, 7:21 p.m., https://x.com/charliekirk11/status/1964469113352573401.

5 Emma Waters, "Protestant Denominations Need Stronger Leadership on Assisted Reproductive Technology," *American Reformer*, January 22, 2024, https://americanreformer.org/2024/01/protestant-denominations-need-stronger-leadership-on-assisted-reproductive-technology.

6 Charlie Kirk (@charliekirk11), "Get married. Have children. Build a legacy. Pass down your values. Pursue the eternal. Seek true joy. Eventually, we will replace the nihilists. [Includes a line graph showing the marriage rate percentage of U.S. adults aged 30–50 from 1939 to 2024, comparing Republicans, Democrats, and Independents.]" *X* (formerly Twitter), last edited July 11, 2024, 1:22 p.m., https://x.com/charliekirk11/status/1811450961975824528.

7 Erika Kirk, "Erika Kirk's Tribute: 'Let Charlie's Miracle Be Your Turning Point,'" *Religion Unplugged*, September 21, 2025, https://religionunplugged.com/news/erika-kirks-tribute-let-charlies-miracle-be-your-turning-point.

Acknowledgments

1 C. S. Lewis, *The Four Loves* (London: Geoffrey Bles, 1960), 65.